SCHOLAST

A PARENT'S GUIDE TO
Reading With Your Young Child

by Dr. Susan B. Neuman & Tanya S. Wright

New York • Toronto • London • Auckland • Sydney • Mexico City • New Dehli • Hong Kong • Buenos Aires

Cover and interior design by Maria Cunningham & David Kepets
Copyright © 2007 by Scholastic Inc.
Printed in U.S.A.

ISBN-13 978-0-439-02420-4
ISBN-10 0-439-02420-X

1 2 3 4 5 6 7 8 9 10   40   13 12 11 10 09 08 07

AGES 0–1

AGES 1–2

AGES 2–3

AGES 3–4

AGES 4–5

The Benefits of Reading Aloud With Young Children...

Singing lullabies, chanting nursery rhymes, acting out fairy tales, sharing bedtime stories—most of us have fond memories of cuddling with a caregiver or snuggling in a parent's lap, all cozied up with a favorite book. The warm feelings associated with these early reading experiences last a lifetime. As parents ourselves, we are eager to re-create this tradition with our own children.

But what child ever imagined that these cozy times with books were important first steps on the road to academic success? Researchers have demonstrated time and time again that reading with young children provides them with the vocabulary, knowledge, and motivation they need in order to achieve in school. How wonderful to know that a cherished time between parent and child is also an integral part of getting children ready for school.

We've written this book to help you make the most out of reading with your young child. The ideas and suggestions we provide about choosing books and reading together are meant to help you enrich the joyous times you spend with your child curled up with great books. We hope you find this guide a helpful companion through the preschool years, as you and your child grow in your love of books.

Benefits of Reading Aloud to Your Child

Most importantly, reading with young children helps them learn to love books. Children whose parents and caregivers read to them regularly understand the joy, the fun, and the knowledge that books can provide. Showing your child the value of books is the single most important thing that you can do to help ensure your child's future educational success. Children who already love books want to learn to read when they are five or six, and eager learners make enthusiastic and successful students. Here are just some of the ways reading will help your child.

Reading Introduces Children to New Ideas and Experiences

Reading with your child provides her with information, experiences, and knowledge. In addition, books are a fantastic way to show children how people interact and to explain why and how things happen.

Although you may live nowhere near an ocean, a book can provide the opportunity for your child to learn about the sea. If you live in a warm place, a book can introduce your child to snow. Books provide limitless opportunities for your child to learn something new.

Reading Helps Children Talk About Their Feelings and Fears

Many parents use books to address their young children's concerns in a non-threatening and comfortable way. Whether you want to help your child make friends, cope with his fear of the dark, or adjust to school, books provide an opportunity to introduce important conversations. It is always easier to begin by discussing what a fictional character is doing or feeling; then you can invite your child to share his ideas and feelings.

Books provide limitless opportunities for your child to learn something new.

Reading Builds Early Language and Literacy Skills

When you read books together, you help your child with language and early literacy development. Infants and toddlers can learn words by listening to you label pictures in a book. In books, preschoolers encounter words that expand their vocabulary beyond the everyday language that they hear in their environment. Understanding words helps children to comprehend increasingly complex books and conversations.

Reading with young children also teaches them about books—both how to use them and why they are useful. Children learn that we read from left to right, they learn which way to turn the pages, and they learn where to find a book's title. Alphabet books help children to recognize letters and learn their sounds. Rhyming books encourage children to listen to the sounds in words. Children develop these little pieces of pre-reading knowledge over time and over many read alouds during their early childhood years.

Reading Together Creates a Close Bond

When you read with your young child, you are also making time to be together in a special way. When you cuddle your child in your arms and focus jointly on a book, you are not only giving your child an invaluable learning experience, but also providing your child one-on-one attention for a few minutes of the busy day.

These are just a few of the great reasons to read with your young child. This book provides specific information about reading with your child at particular ages and stages. How does reading books benefit children of each age? What types of books should you read at each age? What should you do and say? What will your child learn? In this book, you'll find the answers to these questions and many others.

When you read with your young child, you are also making time to be together in a special way.

How to Use This Book

This book is broken down into one chapter for each preschool year from birth to age five, but remember that children develop at different rates. A child's birthday does not result in a dramatic change in the books that she enjoys or in the ways that you read together. In addition to reading the chapter that addresses the age group that your child falls into, it may be helpful to read the chapters on children who are slightly younger and slightly older. You may find that although most of the two-year-old's chapter is appropriate for your child, she is still like a one-year-old in some ways (loves books with simple pictures and one-word labels) and is like a three-year-old in others (is interested in her big sister's alphabet books). ●

Reading With Your Child: Tips for Getting Started

1. Start now! It is never too early to read with your child.

2. Read with enthusiasm. If you are interested, your child will be too.

3. Consider scheduling a regular time for reading that you and your child can look forward to spending together. Many parents read with their children before bedtime.

4. Visit your local library. Children's librarians can help you choose just the right book on almost any topic.

5. Store books within your child's reach. Have the cover face out (rather than the spine) so your child can tell books apart and make choices by the pictures and colors on the cover.

6. Carry a children's book in your baby bag, purse, or briefcase and keep some in your car. Books are a great way to keep your child occupied when you're stuck waiting somewhere.

Reading With Babies

In this chapter...

- **What Babies Learn From Books**
- **Reading With Your Baby**
- **It's Never Too Early to Start**

Babies have so much to learn, and books are a great place to begin. When you hold your baby on your lap and read a book, he will learn that book reading is a special, loving time. Soon you will both look forward to the wonderful experiences that you will have together when you read books. Beyond the quality time you share, your baby will learn many important concepts.

Twinkle, Twinkle, Little Star
by Rosemary Wells

From dinnertime to bath time to bedtime, rituals take on a new sparkle with this delightful rendition of a timeless classic.

Baby Faces
by DK Publishing

Each page of this board book displays a photograph of a baby's face and a label for a different emotion. Babies particularly enjoy looking at faces.

What Babies Learn From Books

Babies can learn a lot from books. When you read a book to your baby, she will listen to the sound of your voice and will begin to respond to your words. Babies particularly enjoy the rhythmic sounds of songs, chants, and nursery rhymes. They love to be bounced or rocked to the rhythm of a song or rhyme. Within a few months, your baby will be able to smile and make cooing noises in response to your words and you'll be able to tell that she is having fun! For time when you don't have the book right in front of you, it is helpful to memorize a selection of chants and nursery rhymes so that you can sing and rhyme with your baby—during a diaper change or a car ride, or on the swings, for instance. It is easy to find the words and music for lullabies and children's songs on the Internet, or you can borrow books and CDs of children's song and verse from the library.

Singing and rhyming are play, but they are also essential activities for helping your baby focus on the sounds of adult language so that he can learn how to talk. In addition, babies begin to learn the meanings of words when you read books. When you point to a picture and say a word, your baby will start to associate the word you say with the picture. By the end of their first year, most babies can understand many words that you say even if they haven't learned to speak yet.

Well-chosen books are stimulating for babies in other ways as well, and babies explore books in many ways. They like to look at the illustrations, particularly if the book contains primary or contrasting colors and clear, simple pictures that stand out from the background of the page. Babies like to grab or swat at the pages of a book to learn about how books feel. As babies grow older, they will be able to grasp and hold a book if it is small enough. Babies also explore everything with their mouths, including books. They often put the sides or corners of books in their mouths to suck or chew. Books provide a wonderful array of sensory experiences that will help your baby to learn about her world.

Black on White
and other books by Tana Hoban

Each page of this board book displays a picture of an object in black against a white background. Babies like to look at these pictures in contrasting colors. There are no words in this book, but it is easy for parents to provide the labels. Also try **White on Black** by the same author.

Reading aloud to babies is an enriching experience with many benefits. Babies can learn to:

1. associate books with warm, close time with a parent or caregiver.

2. listen to language.

3. respond to language.

4. focus on pictures.

5. link words to pictures.

6. practice grasping a book.

7. explore how books taste and feel.

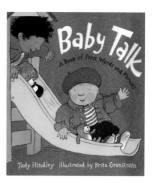

Baby Talk: A Book of First Words and Phrases
by Judy Hindley

This book presents a lively, rhyming tour of a day in the life of a toddler.

AGES 0–1

First Words
by Roger Priddy
Each page of this board book contains a photograph of a common object and is labeled with the correct word. Some babies are particularly attracted to real photographs because they are so vivid. Also try **Animals** by the same author.

Peek-A-Boo, You!
by Roberta Grobel Intrater
Babies will be fascinated by the photographs of other babies making peek-a-boo faces.

Reading Books With Your Baby

Many parents understand that it is important to read with their babies, but they're not sure which books to read or exactly how to read with such a young child. This section provides information to help you feel knowledgeable and comfortable as you begin to read with your baby.

The most important advice is not to worry too much about "getting it right." The suggestions in this book will get you started, but as you and your baby get to know each other, you'll create your own routines and rhythms for reading together that work well for you. Also, remember that book reading should be a fun and relaxing time for you and your baby. Sometimes you may decide to read a book, but your baby may be fussy or uninterested. She may wriggle, swat the book away, or cry. If you sense that it is not a good time to read, it is just fine to put the book away and try again later when you are both ready.

What Type of Books Should I Read?

Certain types of books work best for babies. This section describes the format and content most suitable for babies and suggests some excellent books to get you started.

Format

Because babies like to explore objects with their mouths, you will want to choose books that stand up to this type of wear and tear. Some parents like cloth or vinyl books because they are very sturdy. Board books, which are made of thick cardboard, work well for babies and are more commonly available than vinyl or cloth. Small board books are easy for older infants to grasp with their little hands. Large board books are visually stimulating because the pictures are big and bright. Your baby will benefit from board books of both sizes.

Content

Books with stimulating pictures are ideal for babies. Choose books with large, clear pictures that stand out from the background of the page. Babies like to look at bright, primary colors or distinct black and white images. The language accompanying the pictures should be simple. Books for babies often have one object and a label on each page. Babies love pictures of faces, animals, people, and common objects. Books with these types of images will help your baby learn language as he begins to associate a picture with a word.

Just-Right Books for Babies

The books showcased in this chapter and listed on page 16 provide excellent examples of books that are just right for babies; check the appendix for even more suggestions. You can read them with your young infant, but they will remain interesting to your child well into the second year as she continues to learn to speak and understand new words. Look for other books with characteristics similar to those featured here, but don't feel limited by these suggestions or by the recommended book structure. Books with pictures and labels work well when your baby is alert and ready to learn from books. At bedtime or at other restful times, babies often enjoy listening to books with more words, particularly books that have rhythmic or repetitive language. The rise and fall of adults' voices as they read from almost any book can be very soothing for babies.

Farm Animals
and other books by Lucy Cousins

Each page of this board book contains a picture of an animal and a label. Your baby will love staring at the bright drawings and touching the fuzzy sheep on the cover. Also try **Pet Animals** and **Garden Animals** by the same author.

Hello? Hello?
by Scholastic

A soft, blue-jean cloth book that is shaped like a telephone and features jingle bells in the receiver along with big, puffy wheels.

AGES 0–1

: **My Very First Mother Goose**
: *by Iona Opie*
:
: A collection of over 60 Mother
: Goose rhymes.

: **This Little Piggy and Other**
: **Rhymes to Sing and Play**
: *by Jane Yolen and Will Hillenbrand*
:
: A collection of over 60 lap rhymes,
: songs, clapping rhymes, and finger
: and foot rhymes.

How Should I Read With My Baby?

There's no one right way to read with a baby, but this section will give you some ideas for how to get started.

Find a Comfortable Position

When you're ready to read, hold your baby on your lap and prop him up into a sitting position. Hold the book in front of you so that it is easy for both of you to see.

You can also read books when your baby is lying on his tummy. Prop the book up on the floor so that he can see it when he picks his head up and looks straight ahead. You can sit or lie next to him. Once he is sitting up by himself, you'll be able to hold him on your lap or sit near him on the floor to read. Make sure that the book is within your baby's arm's length, so that he can see it clearly and touch it when he is interested.

Match Your Voice to the Mood

Babies are very focused on the intonation and pitch of adult voices. When you sound happy and excited, they become happy and excited. Make your voice louder and softer or higher and lower to make your baby smile and coo. As you are reading, pay attention to how your baby is responding. Be playful and silly. If she touches a page, or if she laughs and coos at a particular point in the book, stop and read the page over again. It is fine to read a page or the whole book several times in a row, to skip pages, or to look at a particular page for a long time. Reading the same book over and over again helps babies to notice and become familiar with its language.

Let Your Baby Take the Lead

Follow your baby's lead. If he continues to seem interested in a page, let him keep looking at it and you can keep talking about it. If he has lost interest and looks away, you can try tapping the book to draw his attention back to the page. If he's still not interested, you'll know that it is time to move on to a new page.

Allow your baby to grab at the book, to swat the book, to hold the book, and to taste the book. You will have plenty of time to teach him how to treat books properly, but for now he is trying to understand his world by listening, looking, touching, and tasting, and this is a normal and important part of his learning. As he grows, you can help your older infant to learn specific words by pointing to a picture as you say the label or by taking his hand and helping him touch the picture for the word you are saying.

When Should I Read With My Baby?

Reading to your baby every day is important, but exactly when and where is up to you. Some parents and caregivers like to choose a regularly scheduled time to read with their babies. Try to find a time when your baby is typically calm but alert. In addition to reading during an "awake" time, many parents and babies like to read books before bedtime and naps. As you read, the gentle, rhythmic tones of your voice will help your baby to relax and drift to sleep. The routine of reading before bed is one that you can start now and will enjoy together for years to come.

Books can be engaging and exciting or soothing and calming, depending on how you read them and on your baby's mood and schedule. If your baby gets fussy, stop reading and try again at another time. Remember that sharing a book should be an enjoyable experience for both you and your baby. When reading is a close, playful, and special time with caregivers, babies very quickly grow to love books and are eager to spend time cuddled up with you and a book.

Go, Baby, Go!
by Ann R. Blakeslee

Soft, pillowy cloth pages and a sturdy, board-book frame make this book a pleasure for infants to handle. Rhyming text and brightly colored photographs of babies make it even more appealing.

Sweet Dreams
by Kaori Watanabe

This soothing cloth book features fleece blanket on the cover and eight colorful ribbon tags for babies to pull and rub–plus a sweet, rhyming text!

AGES 0–1

My Happy Baby
by Scholastic

This cuddly round cloth book features happy baby animals and six textured fabric petals. Includes a mirror on the back of the book.

Where Should I Read With My Baby?

Some families choose a special place to read—a comfortable chair or a cushion on the floor. You'll probably find that there are many good places to read, and it may be helpful to keep books in a few places so that there is always a book around when you think your baby is interested.

Don't forget that your baby will also enjoy exploring books on her own. Babies like to hold books, and to suck or chew on books, and they particularly love to play with the pages. For infants, books are a special kind of toy, and if they are available, infants will choose to play with them. It's a good idea to keep a few books with your baby's other toys so that she can choose to play with a book. Store books so that the front cover is easily visible to your baby. Soon she will be able to recognize her favorites, and she will choose to play with them or point to books that she wants you to read. This is just another way to help your baby learn to love books and reading.

How Will I Know My Baby Is Learning?

It is hard not to notice that babies are learning—they grow and change so much over their first year of life. If you read to your baby every day, you will see that her response to books will change over the year. At first, she may not really focus on the book, but she will be listening to your voice. She may be soothed by a particular lullaby or by the rhythm of your voice as you read.

Within a few months, she will become much more engaged. She will gaze at the pictures in books and will smile and coo when you make silly or high-pitched sounds with your voice. She may swat at the book when she is excited.

During the second half of her first year, your baby will start to babble. She will make noises that sound as if she is speaking, but the words will not make any sense. She may imitate your voice by babbling while you are reading. There will be times during the day when she is very alert and interactive. You will be able to make her laugh and babble by changing the pitch and intonation of your voice while you read.

By the end of the first year, your baby may point to pictures when she wants you to say a word, she may crawl to get a favorite book that she wants you to read, and she may even try to say words as you point to pictures in a book. When you put her on your lap to read a book, she will know exactly what is going on, and if she wants to read, she will snuggle into your arms and look at the book. She will be happy and excited when you read a favorite book, and she may become fussy when you select a book that is not the one that she wants to read. She may grip the book and throw it just to play or if she is not interested in reading at that moment. Your baby will begin to try to turn the pages, but she probably will only be able to turn several pages at one time, and sometimes she will try to grab the book and hold it while you are reading. All of these behaviors indicate that your baby has started to learn what books are for, she has learned to enjoy books, and her experiences with books are helping her to learn a lot about language.

Is Your Mama a Llama?
by Deborah Guarino
Lloyd the Llama is on a quest to see how many other baby animals have a llama as their mama.

AGES 0–1

It's Never Too Early to Start

It is never too early to introduce your baby to the wonderful world of books! You can start to read to your baby on the day that she is born (and some parents even start to read to their babies before they are born). By the time your baby is born, he has been listening to your voice for months, and when you read to him, he can listen to this soothing and familiar sound. Even during the first few months, when it may seem that your baby is not alert enough to understand or enjoy books, you should start to read together. Positive early experiences with books will help your baby to understand from the very beginning that books are fun, interesting, and exciting, and will start him on the path to a lifetime of learning from books. ●

Books to Read With Your Baby
(AGES 0–1)

Twinkle, Twinkle Little Star
by Rosemary Wells

Baby Faces
by DK Publishing

Black on White
and other books by Tana Hoban

Baby Talk: A Book of First Words and Phrases
by Judy Hindley

First Words
by Roger Priddy

Peek-a-Boo, You!
by Roberta Grobel Intrater

Farm Animals
and other books by Lucy Cousins

Hello? Hello?
by Scholastic

My Very First Mother Goose
by Iona Opie

This Little Piggy and Other Rhymes to Sing and Play
by Jane Yolen and Will Hillebrand

Go, Baby, Go!
by Ann R. Blakeslee

Sweet Dreams
by Kaori Watanabe

My Happy Baby
by Scholastic

Is Your Mama a Llama?
Deborah Guarino

Reading With Your Young Toddler

In this chapter...

- **What Young Toddlers Learn From Books**

- **Reading Books With Your Young Toddler**

- **Books Are Filled With New Words to Learn!**

It is amazing how much children grow and change during their second year. One-year-old children are alert, interested in their world, and highly interactive. They start to walk, which gives them the mobility to explore their environment. Young toddlers also learn to talk, starting with simple first words that describe concrete objects or people around them, for example, *mama* and *dada*. By the time that they are approaching two years of age, most toddlers know lots of words, and they can speak in short, two-word phrases, such as "want mommy." Starting at around 18 months, young toddlers learn words so quickly that they often surprise their parents by using several new words every day.

Trucks

by Byron Barton

Young toddlers enjoy these concept books that provide simple language and pictures on interesting topics.

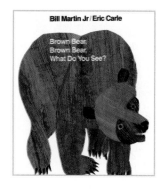

Brown Bear, Brown Bear

by Bill Martin, Jr.

Everyone loves this favorite rhyming book with Eric Carle's vibrant pictures that introduces children to animals and colors.

What Young Toddlers Learn From Books

Reading books is a wonderful way to support your young toddler as she learns words. When you name a picture in a book, you are teaching your toddler new vocabulary. At first, your child will learn to understand that the word you say aloud is connected to the picture in the book, but later she will learn to say the word by herself.

Young toddlers are able to recognize favorite books by their cover, and they will often ask you to read favorites over and over again. Although you may be tired of reading the same book repeatedly, remember that asking for this repetition is your child's way of learning. Every time you read a book, your young toddler learns something new. He wants to learn to understand and to speak, and books are an engaging way for him to gain this new knowledge.

Reading Books With Your Young Toddler

Your child will generally follow your lead during read-aloud time. If you sound excited and playful, your child will be enthusiastic. If you tone of voice is not engaging, your young toddler may look around the room or become wriggly, and he may lose interest in the book. Likewise, if you read in a calm and soothing tone of voice, your reading can help your child to relax and become sleepy.

AGES 1–2

What Type of Books Should I Read?

Young toddlers change dramatically over the course of their second year. This section provides suggestions for the format and content of books that will engage your child during this momentous year.

> Reading to young toddlers is a great way to boost their vocabulary, but it has many other benefits. Young toddlers can learn to:
>
> 1. associate books with playful interaction with a parent or caregiver.
>
> 2. listen to new words.
>
> 3. associate pictures with words.
>
> 4. understand new words.
>
> 5. say new words and phrases.
>
> 6. recognize favorite books by the front cover.
>
> 7. turn the pages of a book.

I Went Walking
by Sue Williams

This book is similar to **Brown Bear, Brown Bear**, but children also enjoy guessing which animal will come next when they see its tail. Flip the page to reveal the entire animal.

Old MacDonald
by Rosemary Wells

This brightly illustrated board book is a delightful version of a popular preschool song.

AGES 1–2

Goodnight Moon
by Margaret Wise Brown
You and your child can say good night to common objects in your child's bedroom with this bedtime classic.

The Mommy Book,
by Todd Parr
Young toddlers adore this book and its companion, **The Daddy Book**, about their very favorite people.

Format

One- to two-year-old toddlers are still very rough with their books, mostly because they do not have the dexterity to hold them or turn the pages gently. Young toddlers may drop books and throw books. They may try to turn the pages in a forceful way. They may still try to suck or chew on books. You can start to teach children of this age that "we are gentle with our books" or "we don't chew on our books," but remember that, at this stage, children still explore the world using all of their senses. Watching a book fly through the air when it is thrown and listening to the sound it makes when it hits the floor are interesting and exciting phenomena for one- to two-year-olds. For all of these reasons, board books remain a good idea at this age. If you can't find a title in board-book format, try to find a hardback cover, and keep a roll of book tape to mend favorite books when they get ripped.

Young toddlers also love lift-the-flap books. They giggle and squeal and are excited to see what is underneath. Children of this age love peek-a-boo. Lift-the-flap provides the surprise of peek-a-boo in book form, and young toddlers can't get enough of reading and playing with this type of book. Children enjoy books such as *Where is Baby's Bellybutton?* by Karen Katz, in which they can lift the sturdy flaps and learn the words for parts of the body. Other types of engineered books, such as pop-up books and books that make noises, are also fun for children of this age.

Content

One- to two- year-old children enjoy simple concept books. These books are about a particular topic, and they have one picture and a label on each page. Reading this type of book helps children learn to associate the word that you say aloud with the picture in the book. Byron Barton's books are excellent examples of concept books that young toddlers adore.

Young toddlers also like books with simple, repetitive language. These books generally feature a repeating sentence; only one word changes on each page, and it refers to the picture. These books often rhyme and have an almost singsong, chant-like feel. *Brown Bear, Brown Bear* by Bill Martin, Jr. and *I Went Walking* by Sue Williams are excellent examples of this type of book; both introduce a new animal on each page.

Books about familiar topics are appealing to young toddlers. Children and parents love Todd Parr's *The Mommy Book* and *The Daddy Book*, which have brightly colored illustrations and simple text about family. *Goodnight Moon* is a classic children's book to read before bedtime. On each page of this rhyming book, you and your child can say good night to a familiar object.

Just-Right Books for Babies

The books discussed above and presented throughout the chapter are a guide, but there are many books that are appropriate for children of this age group; see the appendix for more recommendations. Young toddlers love nursery rhymes and song books. Although children of this age don't really understand stories yet, they may still want to listen to a storybook, particularly if you are reading this type of book to an older sibling.

Different children love different books, and as you explore, you will find the books that your child enjoys. Most important to remember at this age is that one of the goals of reading together is to teach language, so it is ideal to choose books where the connection between the illustrations and the words is simple and clear.

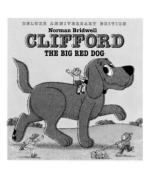

Clifford the Big Red Dog
by Norman Bridwell

As they read this story of Emily Elizabeth's huge red dog, children love to imagine what they could do if they had a dog the size of Clifford.

Bingo
by Rosemary Wells

Children can sing along to their favorite songs and enjoy the sunny illustrations. Includes musical notes for parents.

Read to Your Bunny
by Rosemary Wells

The rhyming text and irresistible illustrations instill in your youngster an early love of reading.

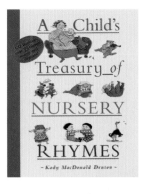

A Child's Treasury of Nursery Rhymes
by Kady MacDonald Denton

A collection of over 100 rhymes, riddles, songs, and lullabies, arranged in four sections by age level (baby, toddler, preschooler, young school-age).

How Should I Read With My Young Toddler?

Young toddlers can be energetic, to say the least. They like to crawl and walk around. They love to use their newfound mobility to explore their world. At times your toddler may want to cuddle on your lap to listen to several stories. At other times, your toddler will be very active, and she won't be able to sit for long. Because young toddlers spend much of their time on the floor (playing and walking), you may want to sit or lie down on the floor with your child to read. Sometimes children are more eager to participate if book reading seems like a continuation of their play on the floor rather than a disruption of their play.

Choose a Book

Create opportunities for your young toddler to make simple choices about which book to read. Providing young toddlers with clear alternatives gives them the opportunity to assert their independence in a productive way. Choose one or two books and place or hold them with the cover forward so that your young toddler can see each book. Children of this age can recognize favorite books by the pictures on the covers. Help your child to make a choice. Say, "Which book should we read? This book? Or this book?" As you mention one of the choices, hold it up or point to it. Say the title because your toddler may remember the familiar language. Your child will learn to point to or grab the book he wants.

Children who are closer to two years old will be able to ask specifically for the book they want, in a simple sentence. They might hold a book up to you and say "Mommy read" or "read book." Praise your child for making a choice: "Good choice! Let's read."

Of course, your young toddler does not always need to be in charge of book selection. At times, he may not make a choice or you may want to introduce a new book. As in other parts of a young toddler's day, book reading and book choice require a balance of routine and flexibility.

Find a Comfortable Position

Always hold or place the book so that your toddler can see, touch, and point to the pictures. As she gets older, she will want to hold the book herself, and she will try to turn the pages. Encourage her as she learns. Help her to hold the book and to turn the pages. As the year progresses, turning the pages in board books will become a little bit easier for her.

Invite Your Toddler to Join In

As you read, you will also need to decide whether to read the book straight through to the end or to watch your toddler's cues and stop when he is interested or curious. There are benefits to both ways of reading. Reading a book all the way through will help your child to learn the patterns of language. He will learn to hear the rhythms and rhymes in the text. As he gets closer to two years old, he will be able to say some of the language with you, and he may even recite book words when he chatters to himself. Reading favorite books over and over again is particularly supportive of this type of learning.

After you have read a book with repeating text several times, help your young toddler to participate. If you are reading Sue Williams's *I Went Walking*, say the refrain, "I went walking, what did you…" Pause and look at your toddler. Encourage him to say *see* with you. By end of second year, children can fill in the blank with you when you read and pause during familiar text. Your child may say several words, such as "what see." Encourage

The Deep Blue Sea: A Book of Colors
by Audrey Wood

Rhythmic, cumulative text adds a new object and color to each picture.

Busy Bath
by Brenda Sexton

In this bath book with colorful animals, children can push the ladybug up and down, squeak the bee, spin the spider, and flip a flap to see a hummingbird come out of its nest.

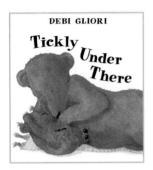

Tickly Under There

by Debi Gliori

This lively text invites toddlers to get to know parts of their bodies.

him ("Good job! What do you see?"), and then keep reading so that he can participate again on the next page.

When you stop to talk more about a particular page or to play games with a book, you are supporting other aspects of your child's language development. Playing "What is that?" or "Where is the...?" games when you look at a picture gives your child an opportunity to practice language and label objects. Sometimes when you read, your child may want to repeat pages or skip pages, or you may spend a lot of time describing one picture to extend your child's language and maintain his interest and attention.

Connect the Book to Your Toddler's Experience

Associating the pictures in a book with real-life objects helps your child to understand that a word can be used beyond the context of the book. For example, when you read *Goodnight Moon*, you could read, "Good night, light," and then point to lights in the room. Say, "Look! There's a light and there's a light. Maria, where is the light?" (help your child to point) "That is a light. Good job! Say good night, light." Use the book as a starting point, but your goal should be to talk, talk, and talk some more. Young toddlers learn language when adults speak to them. The more you engage your child with language, the more she will learn.

When and Where Should I Read With My Young Toddler?

There is no right time or place to read with young toddlers. You can read books throughout the day when your child is interested or you can create a book-reading routine at a particular time of day. No matter when you read during the day, try to make reading a consistent part of your young toddler's bedtime routine.

Store books with your young toddler's toys. It helps young children if books are stored with the cover facing outward, so that they can use the cover art to tell books apart. The pictures on the covers of books have bright, interesting colors, and this makes them an attractive toy for your child to choose if they are readily available. If you store books with toys, your child will choose to play with books independently and will also bring books to you so that you can read.

How Will I Know My Young Toddler Is Learning?

You'll know that book reading is going well when your young toddler chooses to spend time looking at books or asks you to read. Toddlers who are becoming familiar with books look at pages and try to turn them. They'll also repeat single words or two-word phrases that you have just read in the text as well as name lots of objects, many of whose names they'll learn from reading books. When you observe your young toddler, you may notice that he says words or phrases from books when he chatters to himself as he plays independently. You may also hear snippets of book language when you listen to your young toddler on the monitor talking to himself before or after he sleeps. All of these behaviors are evidence that your child is learning from books.

Good Morning, Baby
by Cheryl Willis Hudson

Young toddlers will enjoy reading about the familiar morning routine—waking up, washing, getting dressed, eating, and going out to play.

AGES 1-2

Books Are Filled With New Words to Learn!

This is the year children start to communicate by speaking, and it is amazing to listen to your young toddler use so many new words. Reading books supports her as she continues to learn language. Not only will she listen to and learn to understand new words from books, but now she will be able to repeat and use some of the words that you teach her when you read and talk together.

If you have been reading with your child since she was an infant, you will be building upon these positive early experiences with books. If you have not started to read to your child, now is the perfect time. Young toddlers are attentive and eager to learn, and they grow to understand that reading books is a fun-filled and talk-filled time to spend with parents and caregivers. ●

Books to Read With Your Young Toddler
(AGES 1-2)

Trucks
by Byron Barton

Brown Bear, Brown Bear
by Bill Martin, Jr.

I Went Walking
by Sue Williams

Old MacDonald
by Rosemary Wells

Goodnight, Moon
by Margaret Wise Brown

The Mommy Book
by Todd Parr

Clifford the Big Red Dog
by Norman Bridwell

Bingo
by Rosemary Wells

Read to Your Bunny
by Rosemary Wells

A Child's Treasury of Nursery Rhymes
by Kady MacDonald Denton

The Deep Blue Sea: A Book of Colors
by Audrey Wood

Busy Bath
by Brenda Saxton

Tickly Under There
by Debi Gliori

Good Morning, Baby
by Cheryl Willis Hudson

Reading With Your Older Toddler

AGES 2-3

In this chapter...

- **What Older Toddlers Learn From Books**

- **Reading Books with Your Older Toddler**

- **Enjoy Stories and Learn Language**

Older toddlers love books! Children of this age are interested in everything and they learn language rapidly. Books feed older toddlers' needs for new knowledge and new language. Two-year-olds want to be independent. At the same time, they are attached to their parents and caregivers. One moment, your older toddler is fussing because she doesn't want you to wipe her nose after she sneezes, and a little while later she is calling for you to pick her up and give her a hug. Even the most independent two- to three-year-olds crave the close time with parents and caregivers that book reading provides.

Are You My Mother?
by P. D. Eastman

Introduce your toddler to stories with this book about a baby bird that hatches while its mother is off finding food. The baby goes around asking "Are you my mother?" to various animals until the mother bird returns with food and the two are happily reunited.

Corduroy
by Don Freeman

Older toddlers love the story of Corduroy the teddy bear who searches the store where he lives for a new button so that a little girl will be allowed to buy him. In the end, she decides to buy him and take him home even though he is missing a button.

What Older Toddlers Learn From Books

Book reading will provide you with the opportunity to extend both your child's vocabulary and her ability to construct longer sentences. Older toddlers speak in two- or three-word phrases. Books provide examples of more complete sentences. Additionally, your child's language will develop as she listens to you speak, and your conversations around books will give you lots of opportunities to respond to your child and demonstrate language, especially since she is now able to move beyond labeling books and can enjoy simple stories.

You'll find that reading with your older toddler is lots of fun for both of you. Since your child knows much more language, she will be more interactive than ever during story-reading time. You will both enjoy the opportunity for communication and play that sharing a book provides.

Reading Books With Your Older Toddler

You will be amazed at how much your older toddler already knows about books. She will continue to enjoy books with repetitive, rhyming text. When you read, she will ask simple questions, such as "What that?" and she will respond to your simple questions. When she looks at a book independently, your older toddler will turn the pages and chatter to herself. If you've read a book together often, she may even say some of the words with correct page, matching words to pictures. She will select a book and ask you to read it. All in all, she will be much more actively involved in the reading experience.

What Type of Book Should I Read?

The choices of format and content of books that are appropriate for your child are rapidly expanding. Here are some suggestions on how to choose books perfect for your child's third year.

Older toddlers reap great benefits from being read to. They learn to:

1. receive one-on-one attention from parents or caregivers.

2. enjoy the language and stories in books.

3. listen to and understand simple stories.

4. understand the meaning of new words and phrases.

5. repeat some of the language from books as you read.

6. ask and respond to simple questions about books.

7. turn the pages of a book.

8. choose which book to read.

The Very Hungry Caterpillar
by Eric Carle

Older toddlers learn the days of the week and they learn about how a caterpillar becomes a butterfly. This book is beautifully illustrated with Eric Carle's collages, and it provides lots of interesting information in story form.

When Sophie Gets Angry–Really, Really Angry...
by Molly Bang

Sophie gets mad, climbs a tree to calm down, and is soon ready to come home to her loving family. The bold illustrations reveal the drama of the child's emotions.

AGES 2–3

Clap Your Hands
by Lorinda Bryan Cauley

Your older toddler will enjoy participating in this rhyming and movement book. Read the words and encourage your child to participate by doing the actions.

Mama Loves You
by Caroline Stutson

In this rhyming story, animal mamas—including a porcupine, a honey bear, a polar bear, and a mouse—declare their love for their little ones.

Format

Older toddlers continue to enjoy board books, but they can also begin to use hardcover picture books. They can turn the pages in a standard book but may not have the dexterity to do this gently. Children of this age may rip pages or bend corners as they use these books. The great part of being able to use standard books is that you and your child will now have access to many titles that are unavailable in board-book format.

Content

Older toddlers begin to understand simple stories that have a clear beginning, middle, and end. Usually, these books introduce a character, the character has a simple problem that he goes about solving, and there is always a happy ending. *Are You My Mother?* by P. D. Eastman, is an ideal introduction to this format because it tells a story while still using the repetitive, chant-like text that is familiar to your child from books you're already reading together, such as *Brown Bear, Brown Bear*. In this story, a baby bird hatches while his mother is away finding food. The baby bird looks for his mother. "Are you my mother?" he asks the various creatures that he encounters. In the end, both baby and mother return to the nest, and they are happily reunited. *Corduroy,* by Don Freeman, is another favorite. This book has more text but has a simple storyline that children appreciate. Choose books in which the illustrations help your child understand the story. The pictures should show the action that the words describe to reinforce the meaning of the story.

Older toddlers enjoy information books if the information is provided in story form. *The Very Hungry Caterpillar,* by Eric Carle, is an example of this genre. Children learn how a caterpillar becomes a butterfly, but this information is conveyed through simple narrative text and vibrant, collaged illustrations

Just-Right Books for Older Toddlers

Older toddlers love to mimic adults. They will repeat your actions and your language, and they will repeat the words and phrases they hear in books. Rhyming books help children develop their language skills because their pleasing rhythm and fun sounds encourage children to participate in the reading and to learn the words. Children of this age adore Dr. Seuss books, and they also like to sing songs and recite nursery rhymes. Also try rhyming books that encourage participation and movement. *Clap Your Hands* is a rhythmic chant that you can read while your child follows the instructions in the text and performs the actions. The books featured in this chapter are just-right books for older toddlers; see the appendix for more suggestions.

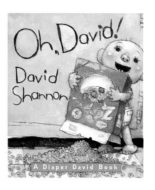

Oh, David!
by David Shannon

A mischievous toddler is scolded for wreaking general havoc, but soon returns to his mother's embrace and a warm "I love you."

Hop on Pop
by Dr. Seuss

Older toddlers enjoy the language in everyone's favorite silly rhyming books. Try **The Cat in the Hat** and **Green Eggs and Ham.**

My Friend Rabbit
by Eric Rohmann

A Caldecott Medal winner. Little rabbit means well, but wherever he goes, trouble follows.

The Little House
by Virginia Lee Burton

A Caldecott Medal winner. A little country house watches as the city slowly encroaches on her peaceful existence.

How Should I Read With My Older Toddler?

Older toddlers do not like to sit for very long. At times, after asking you to read a book, your child may sit for only a few minutes before wriggling off your lap to do something else or to get a different book. She may reach out and turn several pages at once so that you miss part of the story. Try not to become frustrated when this occurs. As she grows, and as you continue to read together, she will be able to focus for longer and longer periods of time.

Choose a Book

Store books so that your child can access them easily. At this age, it is still helpful to keep books near toys so that your child views them as an option when she is playing. Store books with their covers facing outward so that children can identify which book they are choosing. Create opportunities for your child to choose the book that you will read. Children of this age understand simple instructions such as, "go and choose a book for us to read." Older toddlers may find it overwhelming when there are too many books to choose among (for example, when choosing a book from the children's section at a book store or library), but they can make a choice when you provide them with three or four options.

Make the Reading Interactive

When you read together, make sure that the book is held or placed so that your older toddler can see and touch the pages. Encourage her to interact with the book. When you are reading, stop to ask and answer questions. Your older toddler will be able to answer simple questions that you ask as you read, such as "Where does Corduroy live?" or "What is Corduroy looking for?" Questions like this also help you check your child's understanding of the story. If she can't answer, you should. Your answers demonstrate language (how to answer a question), and you will make sure that she comprehends the story by explaining it. Children need lots of support and explanations to help them understand, particularly when you first introduce story books.

Try to expand your child's language by speaking to her in longer sentences. If you're reading *The Very Hungry Caterpillar* and she says, "eat apple," you can extend her language by responding, "You're right. The Very Hungry Caterpillar is eating an apple. Let's see what else he is going to eat."

Encourage your child to participate by pausing during a familiar rhyming book in places where your child is likely to know the words. "I do not like them Sam-I-am. I do not like green eggs and..." At first you will need to help your child to respond by encouraging her to say the missing word with you: "Let's say it together." But soon she will catch on to the game and will excitedly call out the word.

Encourage Toddlers to Read Independently

Give your older toddler time to look at books independently. This can be during play time, before or after naps, or at another time that works with your family's schedule. The goal is for your child to explore books in an unstructured way. She can practice and "play" what she knows by turning pages, looking at pictures, and using language as she "reads."

Food for Thought
by Saxton Freymann and Joost Elffers

Amazing photographs of fruits and vegetables are a fun way to talk about shapes, colors, numbers, letters, and opposites.

You Are Special, Little One
by Nancy Tafuri

Tafuri's gentle words and lush palette express to even the smallest children how very special they are.

AGES 2–3

I Spy Little Animals
by Jean Marzollo and Walter Wick

Rhyming verses ask readers to find hidden objects and toy animals in the beautiful photographs.

When and Where Should I Read With My Older Toddler?

Older toddlers like routines. They feel comfortable, safe, and in control when they know what their day will be like. Consider creating regularly scheduled reading times at least once during the day and again before bed at night. This type of routine helps you both because you know when you will read together, and of course you can always read more often, particularly if your child asks you to read a favorite book.

Older toddlers need lots of time to run around and play outside. Consider reading right after your child finishes more active play. She may be able to sit and focus on a book for a little longer after she has released some energy.

At times your toddler will want to cuddle in your lap for a story. At other times, she will want you to join her on the floor to read. Find a location that works for you and your child so that your older toddler is comfortable and can concentrate on the book that you are reading together.

How Will I Know My Older Toddler Is Learning?

Older toddlers who have been read to since they were infants really understand what books are for. They know to ask you to read when they want to hear a story, and they can choose and request a particular book. Older toddlers are less likely to throw books or to put books in their mouths. Instead, they will look at pictures, turn pages, and chatter as they play with books independently. This change indicates that your child has internalized the purpose of books.

Older toddlers learn lots of language from books. They repeat phrases that you have read. Some children of this age even memorize the language in entire books if they hear them often enough. Watch and listen as your child plays. She may be playing with a stuffed animal, building with blocks, drawing, or sitting in her car seat when she suddenly starts to chant the words from a favorite book.

Most importantly, older toddlers make the transition from books that primarily label objects to books that tell a story. When your child becomes interested in story books, it indicates that her understanding of language has become sophisticated enough for her to follow a simple narrative story. Although she will continue to need lots of explanations and discussion to support her in this transition, the ability to appreciate and understand narratives is an important milestone in your child's language and literacy development.

Big and Little
by Samantha Berger and Pamela Chanko

Each page introduces readers to an adorable photograph of something big and something little, from animals to boats to children. The book features simple, repetitive text that helps young children understand the concepts of little and big.

AGES 2–3

Enjoy Stories and Learn Language

Over this year, the complexity of the language that your older toddler uses and understands develops rapidly. Older toddlers are no longer focused on simply labeling the world around them, but are instead trying to put together longer sentences to communicate. This growth enables older toddlers to appreciate simple stories, and with your support and explanations, your child will be able to enjoy many new books.

Keep reading and keep talking to your older toddler. She is listening, and she is learning from you and from the books that you read together. Don't be surprised when you hear her reciting the words from a book that you've read together frequently. She is paying attention, and she is internalizing the language and knowledge that you are providing. ●

Books to Read With Your Older Toddler
(AGES 2–3)

Are You My Mother?
by P. D. Eastman

Corduroy
by Don Freeman

The Very Hungry Caterpillar
by Eric Carle

**When Sophie Gets Angry –
Really, Really Angry**
by Molly Bang

Clap Your Hands
by Lorinda Bryan Cauley

Mama Loves You
by Caroline Stutson

Oh, David!
by David Shannon

Hop on Pop
by Dr. Seuss

My Friend Rabbit
by Eric Rohmann

The Little House
by Virginia Lee Burton

Food for Thought
by Saxton Freymann and Joost Elffers

You Are Special, Little One
by Nancy Tafuri

I Spy Little Animals
by Jean Marzollo and Walter Wick

Big and Little
by Samantha Berger and Pamela Chanko

Reading With Your Young Preschooler

AGES 3–4

In this chapter...

- **What Young Preschoolers Learn from Books**

- **Reading With Your Young Preschooler**

- **Books Feed Your Curious Child's Mind**

Three- to four-year-old children are curious about everything. They ask lots of questions, and they don't stop asking until they get a satisfactory answer. Books are a terrific way to answer questions, and preschoolers quickly learn that you can find out about almost anything from a book. If your child is interested in dinosaurs, there are lots of informational children's books on dinosaurs. If he likes to help you cook, there are great books with recipes and pictures for children. If he is a fussy eater, there are storybooks with characters who are also fussy eaters, but who learn to try new foods. If your child is learning to count, you can read a counting book together. For almost any question, interest, or struggle that your preschooler poses, you can explore it together in a children's book. Just say, "let's see if we can find a book to read about this..." and it is very likely that after a quick Internet search and a trip to a library or bookstore, you will be reading together on almost any topic of interest. With your help and explanations, your child will be able to apply what he learns in books to his own life.

AGES 3–4

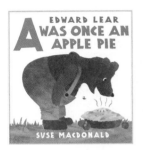

A Was Once an Apple Pie
by Edward Lear, adapted and illustrated by Suse MacDonald

This rollicking alphabet poem will delight young readers with fun-to-read rhymes and bold, hand-painted, cut-paper illustrations.

The Kissing Hand
by Audrey Penn

Each page of this board book displays a photograph of a baby's face and a label for a different emotion. Babies particularly enjoy looking at faces.

What Young Preschoolers Learn From Books

Young preschoolers who were read to when they were infants and toddlers know a lot about books. They have favorite books. They chant the words along with you as your read a book with repetitive or rhyming text. They know that the words in books never change, and if you do not read a favorite book exactly correctly, they will notice and ask you to read it "the real way." Young preschoolers like to look at books by themselves. At times they will look at the pictures, and at other times they will talk to themselves as they look at the pages because they understand that you say words when you read a book.

Young preschoolers know many words, but books are a great way for them to encounter more advanced and interesting vocabulary. Children learn to understand book language when you read a fairy tale or storybook ("and they all lived happily ever after"), and they learn informational vocabulary when you read nonfiction books together.

Reading Books With Your Young Preschooler

Young preschoolers are like sponges. They soak up and store the language and experiences that you provide, and they eagerly ask for more information. They also love to share their newfound knowledge with anyone who is willing to listen. "Guess what…" they say before sharing a story or fact. Reading with your young preschooler is the perfect way to respond to his constant quest for new knowledge.

Young preschoolers love reading and books, which helps them develop their language skills and learn about their world. Specifically, they can learn to:

1. understand that books are filled with lots of information about all sorts of interesting topics.

2. have discussions about the pictures and stories in books.

3. make connections between the experiences of characters in books and their own experiences (with explanations and support from adults).

4. hold books in the right direction and turn pages in the right direction.

5. look at books independently.

6. "read" memorized books or pretend to read books by talking about the pictures.

7. understand that the words in books are the same every time you read them.

8. rhyme.

9. make their own books and become interested in writing.

10. become familiar with storybook language, such as "once upon a time" and "happily ever after."

Five Little Sharks Swimming in the Sea
by Steve Metzger

Wacky rhymes and hilarious illustrations charm preschoolers in this underwater romp.

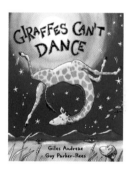

Giraffes Can't Dance
by Guy Parker-Rees

A giraffe who finds his own special music for dancing offers a touching, humorous lesson about the importance of learning how to be yourself.

AGES 3–4

The Snowy Day
by Ezra Jack Keats

A little boy wakes up to find a big snowfall, and he spends the day enjoying the snow.

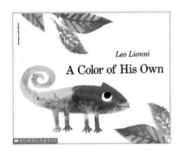

A Color of His Own
by Leo Lionni

A chameleon changes color when he is around new things, but two chameleon friends side by side can be the same color together.

What Type of Book Should I Read?

Young preschoolers enjoy books in almost any format. They may still love the board books that you have been reading together for years, and they may want you to continue reading these. Standard-format hardback books work well too. Preschoolers can even read standard soft cover books, but they will need your help to learn how to treat soft cover books gently and with care. Even when children of this age treat books carefully, at times pages and covers rip, particularly on those best-loved books. If you keep a roll of book tape in the house, you'll be well prepared for this wear and tear.

Reading Stories

Young preschoolers continue to enjoy the illustrations in books. Often in storybooks for children of this age, the illustrations provide additional information that goes beyond the simple story told in the text. The illustrations expand on the story and help children understand it. Storybooks should have a simple and clear narrative structure with a beginning, middle, and end. You should be able to read the entire story in one sitting. Children of this age love stories that are close to their own experiences: books about going to school, making friends, getting along with siblings, or even playing outside on a winter day. They prefer stories that have happy endings, and they strongly dislike scary stories (monsters, bad witches, characters that die).

Exploring Nonfiction

Children of this age also love nonfiction information books with "real pictures" (photographs rather than illustrations). It is difficult to recommend particular nonfiction books because children have varied interests, and you can simply choose books on topics as your child expresses an interest. However, one topic of almost universal interest for children of this age is animals. Children become very interested in bugs, worms, butterflies, sharks, dolphins, horses, dogs, cats, frogs, dinosaurs, rainforest animals, and so on. Choose informational books that are simple and clear. Too much text may be confusing for your child. Even with simple texts, you may need to explain and discuss information to help your child understand. Don't be afraid to choose books with interesting and new vocabulary words. Children of this age like to learn "grown-up" ways to say things.

Building Language and Number Skills

Young preschoolers continue to love books that rhyme or those that have predictable, repetitive language. This type of book encourages young preschoolers to chant along as you read and feel like a participant in the process of reading a book. As the year progresses, older three-year-olds are proud to be able to "read" these memorized books to anyone who will listen.

Children of this age are very interested in counting books and counting chants. Although they often are not yet able to count objects correctly (they may count the same object several times) or to identify the number symbols, they love to practice counting orally. There are many wonderful counting books including *1,2,3, to the Zoo* by Eric Carle and *Ten Black Dots* by Donald Crews. As they approach four years old, young preschoolers become interested in the alphabet. Try *Dr. Seuss's ABC* by Dr. Seuss or *I Spy Little Letters* by Jean Marzollo to get your child excited about learning the alphabet.

Ten Black Dots
by Donald Crews
Learn to count and imagine everything you can make with black dots.

1,2,3 to the Zoo
by Eric Carle
Count the animals as they go on a train to the zoo.

AGES 3-4

There Was an Old Lady Who Swallowed a Fly
by Simms Taback

Sing along and enjoy the funny illustrations in a picture book of this familiar rhyme.

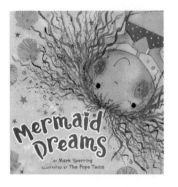

Mermaid Dreams
by Mark Sperring

A daughter shares her day with her mother as she gets ready for bed, with a fun twist for readers at the end when we first see the bottom half of the girl—and discover she's a mermaid!

Just-Right Books for Young Preschoolers

The books featured in this chapter are just a sampling of what appeals to young preschool children. You'll find further suggestions in the appendix, and don't forget to tap your child's teacher, children's librarian, and other parents for ideas.

How Should I Read With My Young Preschooler?

Young preschoolers can typically sit, listen to, and concentrate on a book for about ten minutes at a time before they get wriggly and distracted. Children of this age often want to hold the book while you read and to be in charge of turning the pages.

Reading Nonfiction

For this age group, how to read really depends on the type of book. If you are reading an information book, it will help your child if you stop to explain and discuss new words and new ideas. Help your child with new words by providing a short explanation of what the word means: "When the caterpillar is in its cocoon before it becomes a butterfly, it is called a chrysalis." You don't need to read nonfiction books all the way through, and you can even "look up" information to answer your child's specific questions. When you tell your young preschooler, "That's an interesting question, let's look it up," you are introducing him to the ways that adult readers use informational texts.

Reading Stories

If you're reading a storybook, you may also need to stop and discuss a confusing word or to explain what is happening. You can talk about what might happen next or how a character's experiences are similar to or different from your preschooler's experiences. Although you may stop for conversation, it helps children of this age to read the entire book in one sitting so that they can find out "how it ends."

On the other hand, rhyming books and books with repetitive language should usually be read from start to finish so that your child can listen to the language and learn the rhythm. You may want to pause to let your child participate by filling in a rhyming word or chanting a phrase that occurs throughout the book. In general these books are short and silly, and they help your child listen to and enjoy the sounds of language.

Encourage Young Preschoolers to Read Independently

Children of this age can look at books independently for a short period of time. They like to read in a cozy corner sitting on a pillow or in a special quiet place (under a table or behind a piece of furniture). Young preschoolers also like to look at books with friends. Children may "read" familiar books aloud, and they will even point to the words with their fingers (particularly if they have seen older siblings or friends doing this), but you will notice that there is often a mismatch between the words that they are chanting and the words that are written on the particular page that they are reading. When children pretend to read, they are demonstrating their interest in books and reading. Likewise, when children pretend to write, they are showing their eagerness to learn. Encourage this behavior! Comments like, "You're not really reading" or "Those squiggles don't really say anything" can be hurtful and may discourage your child from voluntarily engaging in these positive and productive preliterate behaviors.

Beach
by Elisha Cooper

The simple magic of building sand castles, collecting seashells, and running from the waves is brought to life through poetic text and lively illustrations.

Red-Eyed Tree Frog
by Joy Cowley

Spectacular close-up color photos and simple engaging text tell the story of a plucky little frog.

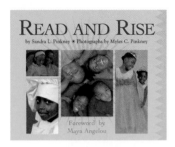

Read and Rise

by Sandra Pinkney

Colorful photographs on bright backgrounds inspire children to dream of possibilities: becoming an astronaut, chef, firefighter, and more. Photos show children reading with adults and on their own, highlighting the importance of reading.

When and Where Should I Read With My Young Preschooler?

At this age, where and when your read depend on you and your child and your particular schedule. Most young preschoolers love reading books with adults, and book reading will remain a special time. Children continue to enjoy the good-night ritual of reading a book before bed.

Remember that ten to 15 minutes is a reasonable amount of time to expect your child to remain engaged. Also, all young preschoolers have days when they just can't sit still (perhaps it is rainy and they haven't been outside to run around). Reading together should be fun, not forced. If your child loves books, he will be eager to read with you later when he has calmed down.

How Will I Know My Young Preschooler Is Learning?

Young preschoolers are typically enthusiastic about books. They will ask you to read a favorite book or choose books to look at all by themselves. There will be times when your preschooler does not feel like reading, but in general he is likely to be interested and curious. He will love to reread favorite books that he knows well, but he will also be excited when you introduce a new book, particularly if the topic is appealing and the pictures are fascinating.

A wonderful thing about young preschoolers is that they will happily tell you what they are learning. They will chatter enthusiastically to you about books and about the information that they learn in books. When you read with your young preschooler, you will also be able to observe his learning. You will see that he understands how to use books when he holds them in the right direction and turns the pages. You will know that he is listening when he chants the words of a book along with you.

Young preschoolers who are read to frequently become interested in writing. They will "write" by drawing scribbles and squiggles, particularly during pretend games when they are pretending to be a grown-up. Your young preschooler may ask you to staple several pages together so that he can make his own book. He may fill this book with squiggles that look like writing as well as pictures, although he probably will not be able to tell you what the book is about. As he approaches four years, or earlier in this year if he has older siblings who can already write, your child may want you to show him how to write his name.

Your young preschooler will be growing towards becoming a reader and a writer. The interest in books that you help to generate every time you read together makes him want to read, and he does "read" by memorizing the words of favorite books or by making up words to go with the pictures. He understands that the writing in books always says the same words, even though he can't read them yet. He knows that alphabet letters are in books, and by the time he is four, he will probably be able to name some letters, even if he is not quite sure what they are for yet. All of these pieces of information about reading will come together later, but for now, when you read aloud with your child, you are providing the building blocks for his future as a reader.

How Do Dinosaurs Play with Their Friends?
by Jane Yolen

Through rhymes and charming illustrations, children will be laughing as they learn valuable lessons about friendship.

AGES 3–4

Books Feed Your Curious Child's Mind

Young preschoolers are eager and interested learners. Children of this age adore books, and they love the special time that they spend with you when you read together. Books provide a way to address your child's constant curiosity. Your young preschooler wants to know and understand, and when you read together, you are helping him and encouraging him in his quest for knowledge. ●

Reading With Your Young Preschooler
(AGES 3–4)

A Was Once an Apple Pie
by Edward Lear; adapted and illustrated by Suse MacDonald

The Kissing Hand
by Audrey Penn

Five Little Sharks Swimming in the Sea
by Steve Metzger

Giraffes Can't Dance
by Guy Parker-Rees

The Snowy Day
by Ezra Jack Keats

A Color of His Own
by Leo Lionni

Ten Black Dots
by Donald Crews

1,2,3 to the Zoo
by Eric Carle

There Was an Old Lady Who Swallowed a Fly
by Simms Taback

Mermaid Dreams
by Mark Sperring

Beach
by Elisha Cooper

Red-Eyed Tree Frog
by Joy Cowley

Read and Rise
by Sandra Pinkney

How Do Dinosaurs Play With Their Friends?
by Jane Yolen

Reading With Your Older Preschooler

AGES 4-5

On some days it is hard to believe that your child is soon going to start kindergarten, but on other days, you know that she is ready. Four-to five-year-old children know so much already, and they are very eager to learn more. They are excited about preschool and friends, they have vivid imaginations and love dramatic play, and they are starting to become interested in learning to read and write. Reading aloud with preschoolers is an essential part of getting them ready for school.

In this chapter...

- **What Older Preschoolers Learn From Books**

- **Reading With Your Older Preschooler**

- **Sharing Books With Your Older Preschooler**

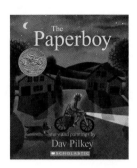

The Paperboy
by Dav Pilkey

The lovely story of a boy and his dog getting up early to deliver the papers while everyone else is asleep.

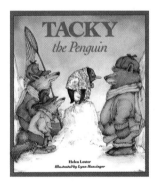

Tacky the Penguin
by Helen Lester

Tacky is an odd bird who is different from the other penguins, but being different helps him to save his penguin friends from hunters.

What Older Preschoolers Learn From Books

When you read rhyming books, older preschoolers can recognize the difference between words that rhyme and words that do not rhyme, and they are learning to distinguish whether two words start with the same sound. This ability to listen to the sounds in words, called phonological awareness, helps children when they try to translate sounds into letters when they are writing and letters into sounds as they learn to read.

Four- to five-year-old children are also capable of having thoughtful conversations about books. They can make reasonable predictions about what will happen next in the story and also make connections between a book and their own lives or other books. They are eager to know whether the stories in books are real or "fake" because they are developing an understanding that some books contain fictional stories while others provide nonfiction information.

Children of this age often ask "why?" Why questions range from those about daily life: "Why do I have to take a bath now?" to more serious subjects, "Why did the hamster die?" Although it's impossible to read a book for each question, books are a great resource for answering them. You can share a book about a character that has a similar experience to one your child is having or find an information book that provides basic information on a topic.

Books continue to be one of the best sources for introducing your child to new and interesting language and vocabulary. In particular, books can help your child to learn words that she may not encounter in everyday conversation. Books may introduce language that is conceptual rather than concrete by addressing topics such as feelings, imagination, or fairness.

Older preschoolers are poised to enter school. Continuing to read to them helps them learn to:

1. understand new information.

2. become interested in and excited about learning to read and write all by themselves.

3. make up their own stories.

4. make connections between book characters' experiences and their own experiences.

5. compare characters and stories across different books

6. learn abstract language beyond the language that they use in everyday conversation.

7. understand new and interesting vocabulary.

8. recognize the alphabet and learn some of the letters' sounds.

9. develop phonological awareness, the ability to hear and distinguish the sounds in our language.

10. recognize the front of the book and the back of book, and know where to find the title of the book and the name of the author.

11. hold a book in the right direction, turn pages, be able to point to which way to read (left to right, top to bottom), and to know where to go next at the end of a line.

Will I Have a Friend?
by Miriam Cohen

Jim is worried about whether or not he will have a friend at school. Jim makes a friend and they make plans to play together the next day.

Wemberly Worried
by Kevin Henkes

Wemberly worries about everything, including starting school. When her teacher introduces her to a friend, Wemberly stops worrying about school and is eager to return the next day.

Dear Juno

by Soyung Pak

Juno wants to write a letter to his grandmother in Korea, but he doesn't know how to write. Juno learns that he can communicate with his grandmother by sending pictures.

The Magic Rabbit

by Richard Jesse Watson

A very unusual rabbit discovers the wonders of a mysterious hat—and his own imagination.

Reading Books With Your Older Preschooler

Four- to five-year-old children are continually moving toward becoming independent readers and writers. When you read with your older preschooler, you help her in this process. You teach her how to use books and you teach her that books are wonderful resources for knowledge and for fun. Children who have learned to love books are excited to learn to read and write "all by themselves," and this enthusiasm can help to facilitate a smooth transition into the elementary school years.

What Types of Book Should I Read?

Preschoolers' interests are broader than they've ever been, and the range of books open to them is expanding. They can enjoy books in any format—from board books to softcover. Try exploring the following types of books.

Storybooks

Children of this age can read standard picture books. They enjoy storybooks with multiple episodes that follow a simple narrative structure. Children love books that are funny or silly, and they like logical and happy endings. Preschoolers have rich imaginations, and they enjoy stories about everyday occurrences that slip into the ridiculous. They also enjoy fairy tales and fantasy books and may be interested in fairies, princes and princesses, and superheroes.

Books That Address Children's Feelings and Fears

Many four- to five-year-old children have real apprehensions and fears that range from concerns about school to worries about monsters under the bed, and storybooks are a helpful way to begin conversations about your child's concerns. For example, *Will I Have a Friend?* by Miriam Cohen tells the story of a boy who wonders whether he will make friends when he starts kindergarten.

Alphabet Books

Older preschoolers love alphabet books and books with repetition and rhyme. Your child will want to read books that you read together when she was younger, but now she will chant along with you as you read. Children of this age also continue to enjoy counting books and chants.

Wordless Picture Books

Introduce your child to wordless books and encourage her to tell you a story. *Pancakes for Breakfast* by Tomie dePaola is a wonderful way to get started. The pictures are vivid and interesting, but the story is easy to follow. The pictures will guide your child toward telling a story that has a beginning, middle, and end.

Information Books

Older preschoolers enjoy information books of all types. They are particularly attracted to books that include vivid photographs or interesting illustrations. Information books are a wonderful way to help your child learn fascinating information as well as new vocabulary. Preschoolers often become fixated on a particular topic and want to read every book that they can find on it.

Just-Right Books for Older Preschoolers

There are countless children's books that are appropriate for four-year-old children. The books featured throughout this chapter offer just a starting point; you'll find additional suggestions in the appendix. If you are looking for a book on a particular topic, search the Internet, speak to a children's librarian, talk to your child's preschool teacher, or ask other parents.

Alligator Baby
by Robert Munsch

Kristen's mother has a baby at the zoo rather than at the hospital. Her parents mistakenly bring home animals from the zoo rather than her baby brother. Kristen saves the day by rescuing her new baby brother from the zoo.

Koko's Kitten
by Dr. Francine Patterson

The true story of a gorilla that communicates in sign language and her friendship with a kitten.

AGES 4–5

Eight Silly Monkeys
by Steve Haskemp

Count backwards from eight by chanting this familiar rhyme. Touch the plastic monkeys through the pages.

Pancakes for Breakfast
by Tomie dePaola

Make up your own story about gathering ingredients and making pancakes.

How Should I Read With My Older Preschooler?

You will want to read differently with your older preschooler depending on the type of book that you are reading. Storybooks should be read all the way through in one sitting, but you can stop for discussion as necessary. You don't need to read the entire book when you are reading an informational text; you can just look up the answer to a specific question. Rhyming books should be read all the way through so that your child can experience the rhythm of the language. Ten to fifteen minutes is a reasonable amount of time for your child to be able to sit and concentrate on a story. Here are some more guidelines for reading with preschoolers.

Get Into Character

Older preschoolers love silliness and they will laugh and laugh if you "ham it up" as you read. Use different voices for the characters and do hand motions. You can even act out the story together. Nothing is funnier and more entertaining for a four- to five-year-old child than an adult acting ridiculous.

Encourage Preschoolers to Ask Questions

Four- to five-year-olds can also tell you when they don't understand. Encourage your child to ask questions as you read. Teach her to say, "What does that mean?" if she doesn't understand a word so you'll know when it is time to stop and explain.

Invite Preschoolers to Participate

At this age, you can encourage your child to participate as you read, but try not to be too pushy. Preschoolers are beginning to be interested in reading, but they can become resistant if this means missing out on the fun of simply listening to a story. Gentle suggestions such as, "do you want to be my helper while we read today?" prompt your child to participate but allow her an "out" if she just wants to listen. Your child can help by turning pages, "reading" the parts of the book that she has memorized, finding letters of the alphabet, or pointing to the words while you read. If your child wants to point to the words, you can gently guide her hand at first, to show her how you read along the lines. Later, let her point by herself as you read the words. This helps her to see how we read from left to right across the page, and that words are separated by spaces, and it may help her to notice specific words.

Give Preschoolers Time to Read on Their Own

Four- to five-year-old children also need time to look at books by themselves. After you've finished reading together, consider giving your child a few extra minutes before turning off the lights to "read" by herself before naps or bedtime.

When and Where Should I Read With My Older Preschooler?

There is no right time or place to read with your preschooler. Some families have routine story times, and others read when the moment seems right. It is most important that you read to your child regularly, at least once a day.

How Will I Know My Older Preschooler Is Learning?

Most four- to five-year-olds are excited to spend time reading with adults. As at any age, there may be times when you want to read, but your child does not. However, in general, older preschoolers are enthusiastic and eager when adults suggest reading a story, and the experience helps them build skills and knowledge they'll use in kindergarten and beyond.

Observe Children at Play

As preschoolers learn new things, their knowledge enters into their pretend play. Your older preschooler may pretend that he is a character from a story that you have read together. For instance, he may be a mommy cat taking care of kittens (after reading a book about baby animals at school). Play with friends or alone is how older preschoolers process and extend their learning; it helps them try out what they know in a safe and comfortable way.

My Five Senses
by Aliki

Children learn about the five senses in this informative book that answers questions such as "How do the senses work?" and "How do our senses help us?"

The Graphic Alphabet
by David Pelletier

This book asks readers to determine the letter from the picture and one-word clues. It provides lots of opportunities to talk about letters and words.

AGES 4–5

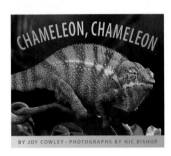

:   **Chameleon, Chameleon**
:   *by Joy Cowley*
:
:   Experience close up the many
:   moods and colors of chameleons
:   as one cautious chameleon braves
:   many dangers in search of a new
:   home.

Encourage Early Reading and Writing

You will notice that your older preschooler is becoming more and more independent with books. Although she still loves to listen to you read stories (and will enjoy this well into her late elementary school years), she can also chant along with you as you read, and she can "read" memorized books by herself.

By the time she is five, she will probably be able to recognize most letters of the alphabet. Alphabet books will have helped her to learn words that start with some of the letters, and she will notice letters in the environment. Perhaps your child knows that a stop sign says "stop," or she recognizes her sibling's name when she sees it on a piece of paper in your house. Four-year-olds learn to write their names in uppercase letters, and they can spell out the letters in their names: "My name is Rachel. R-A-C-H-E-L."

Children who have been read to over their first four years love to make their own special books from several pieces of paper stapled together. When they create their own books, older preschoolers write strings of letters (or shapes that look close to letters) rather than squiggles. As they approach five years old, some older preschoolers may be able to label pictures with letters that make sense, usually the first sounds in important words. They may write *IWP* for "I went to the park." If your child does this type of writing, encourage her! She is using her knowledge of the alphabet to write, and this indicates that she is starting to understand how letters work. Children of this age also "write" in their pretend play and they love to make cards and notes.

By the time she is five, your child will probably be able to rhyme, and she will think it is very funny to make up nonsense rhyming words, which is an important prereading skill.

Get Your Child Talking About Books

While you read a book, you will be able to engage your older preschooler in conversations about the story. Say, "Do you think that could really happen? Why? Why not?" or "Wow! This is exciting. What do you think is going to happen next?" or "I wonder how Tacky is feeling. What do you think?" Your child's responses to

AGES 4–5

these questions, and the discussions that these questions spark, are a marker of your child's more sophisticated ability to interact with books

Sharing Books With Your Older Preschooler

Encourage your older preschooler's interest in books by letting her help you as you read. Praise her for her contributions but understand if sometimes she wants to sit back and enjoy a story while you read. The books that you have shared throughout her early childhood years have sparked her interest in reading and have helped her to become an enthusiastic learner. These strengths will serve her well as she makes the transition to elementary school. ●

Nacho and Lolita
by Pam Munoz Ryan

A beautifully told and illustrated story of two birds from very different places that proves any difference can be overcome with love.

Reading With Your Older Preschooler
(AGES 4–5)

The Paperboy
by Dav Pilkey

Tacky the Penguin
by Helen Lester

Will I Have a Friend?
by Miriam Cohen

Wemberly Worried
by Kevin Henkes

Dear Juno
by Soyung Pak

The Magic Rabbit
by Richard Jesse Watson

Alligator Baby
by Robert Munsch

Koko's Kitten
by Dr. Francine Patterson

Eight Silly Monkeys
by Steve Haskemp

Pancakes for Breakfast
by Tomie dePaola

My Five Senses
by Aliki

The Graphic Alphabet
by David Pelletier

Chameleon, Chameleon
by Joy Cowley

Nacho and Lolita
by Pam Munoz Ryan

AGES 0–1

Books for Babies

AGES 0–1

Agard, J. *Wriggle Piggy Toes*. Frances Lincoln.

Aigner-Clark, J. *Water, Water, Everywhere*. Baby Einstein Co.

Alborough, J. *Hug*. Candlewick Press.

Arma, T. *Little Grown-Ups* and *Water Babies*. Grosset & Dunlap.

Ashman, L. and Dryer, J. *Babies On The Go*. Harcourt.

Asim, J. *Whose Toes Are Those?* and *Whose Knees Are These?* Little, Brown.

Baby Faces. DK Publishing.

Baicker, K. *Snuggle Me Snuggly!*, *Wake-Ity Wake!* and *Yum Tummy Tickly!* Handprint Books.

Baker, K. *Little Green*. Harcourt.

Barritt, M. *Hickory Dickory Dock*. Handprint Books.

Beaumont, K. *Baby Danced the Polka*. Dial.

Blackstone, S. *Bear In Sunshine*. Barefoot Books.

Blake, M. *Off To Bed* and *Out To Play*. Candlewick Press.

Blakeslee, A. *Go, Baby, Go!* and *Play, Baby, Play*. Scholastic.

Boynton, S. *Dinosaur's Binkit*, *Moo Cow Book*, and *My Puppy Book*. Little Simon.

Boynton, S. *Hey, Wake Up!* and *Pajama Time*. Workman Publishing Co.

Browne, A. *My Mom*. Farrar, Straus & Giroux.

Buller, J. *I Love You, Good Night*. Little Simon.

Butler, J. *Whose Baby Am I?* Viking.

Calmenson, S. *Welcome, Baby*. HarperCollins.

Campbell Ernst, L. *Breakfast Time*. Blue Apple.

Carle, E. *My Very First Book of Shapes*. Philomel.

Chorao, K. *The Baby's Good Morning Book* and *The Baby's Playtime Book*. Dutton.

Christian, C. *Where Is the Baby?* Star Bright.

Cimarusti, M. *Peek-A-Pet*. Dutton.

Cousins, L. *Farm Animals*. Walker Books, Ltd.

Cousins, L. *Snacktime, Maisy!* Candlewick Press.

Cowley, J. *Mrs. Wishy-Washy*. Philomel.

Curlee, L. *Ballpark: The Story of America's Baseball Fields*. Simon & Schuster.

Downes, B. *Baby Days: A Quilt of Rhymes and Pictures*. Candlewick Press.

Dunrea, O. *Gossie & Friends*. Houghton Mifflin.

Dyer, J. *Animal Crackers*. Little, Brown Young Readers.

Emberley, R. *My City/Mi ciudad*, *My Garden/Mi jardin*, *My Room/Mi cuarto*, and *My School/Mi escuela*. Little, Brown.

Filipowich, B. *My Ducky*. Innovative Kids.

Four Seasons. DK Publishing.

Frazee, M. *Walk On! A Guide for Babies of All Ages*. Harcourt.

Fujikawa, G. *Babies*. Grosset & Dunlap.

Good Night, Baby. DK Publishing.

Got, Y. *Sam's Little Sister* and *Sam Loves Kisses*. Chronicle.

Grobel Intrater, R. *Eat! / ¡Qué rico!*, *Hugs & Kisses / Besitos Y abrazos*, *Peek-A-Boo / ¡Cucú!*, *Sleep! / Dulces sueños*, *Smile! / ¡Sonríe!*, and *Splash!/ ¡Al agua, patos!* Scholastic.

Guarino, D. *Is Your Mama a Llama?* (Audio). Scholastic.

Guettier, B. *Dinosaurs*. Kane/Miller.

Gutman, A. *Daddy Cuddles* and *Mommy Loves*. Chronicle.

Hathon, E. *Oh Baby – A Touch-And-Feel Book*. Grosset & Dunlap.

Herman, R.A. *Jack and Jill* and *The Little Piggy Went To Market*. Handprint Books.

Hindley, J. *Baby Talk*. Candlewick Press.

Hoban, T. *Black on White*. Greenwillow.

Horaek, P. *Bird, Fly High!* Candlewick Press.

Jenkins, E. *Hug, Hug, Hug!* and *Num, Num, Num!* Farrar, Straus & Giroux.

Jolley, M. *I'll See You in the Morning*. Chronicle.

Julian-Ottie, V. *My Name Is Lucy*. Gingham Dog Press.

Katz, K. *Where Is Baby's Belly Button?* and *Where Is Baby's Mommy?* Little Simon.

Keillor, G. *Daddy's Girl*. Hyperion.

Klinting, L. *What Do You Want?* Groundwood Books.

Krauss, R. *Goodnight Goodnight Sleepyhead*. Harper Collins.

Kubler, A. *The Wheels on the Bus*. Child's Play International Ltd.

Kunhardt, E. *Bunny's Bath Time*. Rebound.

Lacome, S. *Sleep, Baby, Sleep*. Silver Dolphin.

Lawler, J. *If Kisses Were Colors*. Dial.

Lee, S. *Please, Baby, Please*. Simon & Schuster.

Linenthal, P. *Look at the Animals!* Dutton.

Lionni, L. *Let's Play*. Knopf.

Mantegazza, G. *What Am I?* Edaf.

Mavor, S. (Ill.) *Hey, Diddle, Diddle!* and *Mary Had A Little Lamb*. Houghton Mifflin.

Mayhew, J. *Cluck, Cluck, Who's There?* The Chicken House.

McMullan, K. *Baby Goose*. Hyperion.

AGES 1–2
Books for Young Toddlers

McMullan, K. *If You Were My Bunny*. Scholastic.

Milord, S. *Love That Baby*. Houghton Mifflin.

Miura, T. *Ton*. Chronicle.

My First Word Book. DK Publishing.

Nash, S. *The Snuggliest Snuggle In The World*. Gingham Dog Press.

Neusner, D. *Clifford Touch-and-Feel Day*. Scholastic.

Ochiltree, D. *Lull-a-Bye, Little One*. Putnam.

O'Connell, R. *The Baby Goes Beep*. Roaring Brook.

Opie, I. *My Very First Mother Goose*. Candlewick Press.

Pan, H. *Piggy In My Pocket* and *What's In Grandma's Grocery Bags?* Star Bright.

Patricelli, L. *Blankie* and *Binky*. Candlewick Press.

Pearson, T.C. *Little Miss Muffet* and *Diddle, Diddle, Dumpling*. Farrar, Straus & Giroux.

Pinkney, B. *Hush, Little Baby*. Amistad.

Piper, W. *Baby's Little Engine That Could*. Grosset & Dunlap.

Priddy, R. *First Words*. Priddy Books.

Raschka, C. *Five for a Little One*. Simon & Schuster.

Raschka, C. *Goosey Goose*. Hyperion.

Root, P. *Hop!* Candlewick Press.

Rosen, M. *Michael Rosen's Sad Book*. Candlewick Press.

Ross, K. *The Little Noisy Book*. Random House.

Ross, T. *Lucy Wants to Help* and *Lucy Wants to Play*. Parklane.

Saltzberg, B. *Goodnight Kisses*. Red Wagon/Harcourt.

Sami. *Baby Animals* and *Baby Talk*. Blue Apple.

Schulman, M. *Amazing Animals, Jazzy Jobs, Super Sports*, and *Wacky Weekend*. Sterling.

Shannon, D. *Good Boy, Fergus* and *Oh, David!* Scholastic.

Silverstein, S. *Runny Babbit*. HarperCollins.

Stockham, J. *Down by the Station*. Child's Play International Ltd.

Su-Kennedy, H. *What Do I Do?* Viking.

Taback, S. *Simms Taback's Big Book Of Words, Where Is My Friend?* and *Where Is My House?* Blue Apple.

Thompson, L. *Little Quack's Bath Book*. Little Simon.

Tornek, A. *Rainbow Ride*. Price Stern Sloan.

Touch–and–Feel Kitten. DK Publishing.

Van Der Put, K. (Ill.) *Little Ladybug*. Chronicle.

Van Laan, N. *Tickle Tum!* Aladdin.

Walsh, M. *Do Lions Live on Lily Pads?* Houghton Mifflin.

Watanabe, K. *Sweet Dreams*. Scholastic.

Weeks, S. *Overboard*. Harcourt.

Wells, R. *Carry Me!* and *McDuff's Favorite Things*. Hyperion.

Wells, R. *I Love You A Bushel and A Peck*. HarperCollins.

Wells, R. *The Itsy Bitsy Spider* and *Twinkle, Twinkle, Little Star*. Scholastic.

Williams, S. *Let's Go Visiting*. Voyager Books.

Winburn, W. *Teddy Bears, Teddy Bears*. Sterling.

Wolff, A. *Me Baby, You Baby*. Dutton

Wright, B.F. *The Real Mother Goose* and *The Real Mother Goose Classic Color Rhymes*. Scholastic.

Yolen, J. *This Little Piggy* and *Other Rhymes to Sing and Play*. Candlewick Press.

Ziefert, H. *Woof-Woof* and *Zoo Parade!* Blue Apple.

AGES 1–2

Adams, D. *Zoom*. Peachtree.

Ahlberg, J., & Ahlberg, A. *Each Peach Pear Plum*. Viking.

Alborough, J. *Tall*. Candlewick Press.

Allen, J. *I'm Not Cute*. Hyperion.

Allen, K. *Slide, Already!* Houghton Mifflin.

Arnold, M. *Roar of a Snore*. Dial.

Barton, B. *Trains*. Harper Festival.

Benjamin, A.H. *A Duck So Small*. Little Tiger Press.

Berenstain, S. & J. *My New Bed*. Random House.

Bergman, M. *Snip Snap! What's That?* HarperCollins.

Blair, M. *The Up and Down Book*. Golden Books.

Boelts, M. *Little Bunny's Pacifier Plan*. Albert Whitman & Company.

Bolam, E. *Cat Goes Fiddle-I-Fee*. Sterling.

Bond, F. *Tumble Bumble*. Harper Festival.

Brandon, A. *Moving Day*. Green Light Readers.

Brodsky, E. & Lubell, R. *Sophie & Benjamin Watch a Train Go By*. Harper Festival.

Brown, L. *How to Be*. HarperCollins.

Brown, M.W. *Big Red Barn*. Harper Festival.

Brown, R. *Old MacDonald Had a Cow*. Sterling.

Butterfield, M. *Peek-A-Who?* Scholastic.

Carle, E. *Have You Seen My Cat?* Aladdin.

Carlson, N. *Get Up and Go*. Viking.

Chorao, K. *The Baby's Lap Book*. Dutton.

Christelow, E. *Five Little Monkey's Sitting in a Tree*. Clarion.

Books for Young Toddlers

Christian, C. *Where's the Kitten?* Star Bright.

Cousins, L. *Maisy Goes Camping.* Candlewick Press.

Cowell, C. *What Shall We Do With the Boo-Hoo Baby?* Scholastic.

Cowley, J. *Mrs. Wishy Washy's Scrubbing Machine.* Philomel.

Crews, D. *Freight Train.* Greenwillow.

Cronin, D. *Wiggle.* Atheneum.

Degen, B. *Jamberry.* Harper Collins.

Denslow, S.P. *In the Snow.* Greenwillow.

Denton, K. *A Child's Treasury of Nursery Rhymes.* Kingfisher Books.

Dewan, T. *Bing: Bed Time.* David Fickling.

Dotlich, R. *Grandpa Loves.* HarperCollins.

Dunbar, J. *Shoe Baby.* Candlewick Press.

Dwight, L. *Brothers and Sisters.* Berkley.

Dyer, J. *Little Brown Bear Won't Take a Nap.* Little, Brown.

Elgar, R. *Where's My Dinner?* Egmont Books.

Fisher Wright, B. (III). *My First Real Mother Goose Board Book.* Scholastic.

Fleming, D. *The Everything Book.* Henry Holt & Co.

Fox, M. *Where Is the Green Sheep?* Harcourt.

Frazee, M. *Walk on: A Guide for Babies of All Ages.* Harcourt.

Freymann, S. *Baby Food* and *Fast Food.* Scholastic.

Gleeson, L. *Cuddle Time.* Candlewick Press.

Gliori, D. *Bedtime Stories.* DK Children.

Gliori, D. *Can I Have a Hug?* Scholastic.

Grace, W. *Red Train.* Scholastic.

Grossnickle Hines, A. *My Own Big Bed.* Greenwillow Books.

Harper, D. *Sit, Truman.* Harcourt.

Hello? Hello? Scholastic.

Herman, R.A. *Pat-a-Cake.* Handprint Books.

Hill, E. *Where's Spot?* Putnam.

Holloway, Z. *Colors.* Scholastic.

Hughes, S. *Dogger.* HarperCollins.

Hunter, J. *I Can Do It.* Frances Lincoln.

Isadora, R. *What a Family.* Putnam.

Jenkins, S. *Move.* Houghton Mifflin.

Jocelyn, M. *One Some Many* and *Over Under.* Tundra.

Johnson, A. *Joshua by the Sea.* Scholastic.

Katz, K. *Best Ever Big Brother.* Grosset & Dunlap.

Katz, K. *Ten Tiny Tickles.* Simon & Schuster.

Katz, K. *Where Is Baby's Belly Button?* Little Simon.

Krauss, R. *Bears.* Harper Collins.

Kuskin, K. *Under My Hood I Have a Hat.* Harper Collins.

Larranaga, A.M. *Popo and Lolo Are Friends* and *Popo and Lolo and the Red Apple.* Candlewick Press.

Lenski, L. *Spring Is Here.* Random House.

Lewis, K. *My Truck Is Stuck* and *Lot at the End of the Block.* Hyperion.

Lord, J. *Here Comes Grandma!* Holt.

Macdonald, S. *Edward Lear's A Was Once an Apple.* Orchard.

Martin, B. *Brown Bear, Brown Bear.* Holt, Rinehart & Winston.

Martin, B., Jr. *"Fire! Fire!" Said Mrs. Mcguire.* Harcourt.

Mayo, M. *Dig Dig Digging.* Henry Holt & Co.

McBratney, S. *Bedtime Stories.* Kingfisher Books.

McCurry, K. *Farm Babies.* Northword Press.

McPhail, D. *Favorite Tales.* Scholastic.

Milgrim, D. *Time to Get Up, Time to Go.* Clarion.

Noisy Farm. DK Publishing.

Numeroff, L. *If You Give a Mouse a Cookie.* Harper.

Ohi, R. *Pants Off First.* Fitzhenry & Whiteside, Ltd.

Omerod, J. *Sunshine.* Frances Lincoln.

Oxenbury, H. *I See.* Candlewick Press.

Parr, T. *The Feel Good Book.* Megan Tingley.

Patricelli, L. *Binky.* Candlewick Press.

Peck, R. *Monster Night at Grandma's House.* Dial.

Pingry, P.A. *San Diego Zoo Baby Tiger.* Candy Cane Press.

Pinkney, B. *Hush, Little Baby.* Greenwillow.

Prince, A.J. *What Do Wheels Do All Day?* Houghton Mifflin.

Provost, E. *Ten Little Sleepyheads.* Bloomsbury.

Rathman, P. *Good Night, Gorilla.* Putnam.

Reasoner, C. *Whose House Is This?* Price Stern Sloan.

Redding, S. *Up Above & Down Below.* Chronicle.

Ricklen, N. *Mommy and Me.* Little Simon.

Robert, Y. *Red Tractor.* Golden Books.

Rosetti, C. *Sing Song: A Nursery Rhyme Book.* Viking.

Serrano, E. *Leo and His Dog Lou.* Hardenville.

Sexton, B. (III). *Busy Bath.* Scholastic.

Shannon, D. *David Smells* and *Good Boy, Fergus!* Scholastic.

Shaw, N. *Sheep in a Jeep.* Houghton Mifflin.

Slater, D. *Baby Shoes.* Bloomsbury.

Smee, N. *Funny Face.* Bloomsbury.

Sperring, M. *The Fairy Tale Cake.* Scholastic.

Books for Older Toddlers

Stiegemeyer, J. *Cheep! Cheep!* Bloomsbury.

Suen, A. *Red Light, Green Light.* Gulliver Books.

Taber, T. *Rufus At Work.* Walker Books.

Thomas, F. *Little Monster's Book of Numbers* and *Little Monster's Book of Opposites.* Bloomsbury.

Thompson, L. *Little Quack's Bedtime.* Simon & Schuster.

Tong, W. *My Toys.* Andrew McMeel Publishing.

Tucker, S. *Colors.* Simon & Schuster.

Tyler, A. *Timothy Tugbottom Says No.* Putnam.

Vere, E. *Everyone's Sleepy.* Scholastic.

Voake, C. *Hello Twins.* Candlewick Press.

Walker, A. *There Is a Flower at the Tip of My Nose Smelling Me.* HarperCollins.

Warabe, K. *Baby Animals* and *Zoom Zoom.* Flipflop Books.

Watanabe, K. (Ill.) *I Love You.* Scholastic.

Weeks, S. *Overboard!* Harcourt.

Wells, R. *Old MacDonald, Read to Your Bunny,* and *The Bear Went Over the Mountain.* Scholastic.

Whitford, R. *Little Yoga.* Henry Holt.

Wick, W. *Can You See What I See: Seymour Makes New Friends.* Scholastic.

Williams, S. *I Went Walking.* Red Wagon Books.

Willis Hudson, C. *Good Morning, Baby* and *Good Night, Baby.* Scholastic.

Wilson, K. *Bear Wants More.* Margaret K. McElderry.

Wilson-Max, K. *This Is the Way We Take a Bath.* Scholastic.

Winthrop, E. *Shoes.* Harper Trophy.

Wolff, F. *It Is the Wind.* HarperCollins.

Wood, A. *The Deep Blue Sea: A Book of Colors.* Scholastic.

Yaccarino, D. (Ill). *Five Little Ducks.* Harper Festival.

Yang, J. *Joey and Jet.* Atheneum.

Yolen, J. *Baby Bear's Books.* Harcourt.

Young, E. *My Mei Mei.* Philomel.

Ziefert, H. *Noisy Barn* and *Noisy Forest.* Blue Apple.

AGES 2–3

Abrams, P. *Now I Eat My ABC's.* Cartwheel Books.

Agee, J. *Terrific.* Hyperion.

Alborough, J. *Duck in the Truck.* Harper.

Alexander, M. *Lily and Willy.* Candlewick Press.

Aliki. *Hush Little Baby.* Prentice-Hall.

Aliki. *My Five Senses.* Harper Trophy.

Anno, M. *Anno's Alphabet.* Crowell.

Apperley, D. *Good Night, Sleep Tight, Little Bunnies.* Scholastic.

Archambault, J., & Martin, B. *Chicka Chicka Boom Boom.* Simon & Schuster.

Arnold McCully, E. *School.* Harper Collins.

Arnold, T. *Five Ugly Monsters.* Scholastic.

Bajaj, V. *How Many Kisses Do You Want Tonight?* Little, Brown Young Readers.

Bang, M. *When Sophie Gets Angry – Really, Really Angry...* Scholastic.

Bates, I. *Five Little Ducks.* Scholastic.

Benjamin, A. *Rat-a-Tat, Pitter Pat.* Harper.

Berenstain, S. & J. *The Berenstain Bears Go to the Doctor.* Random House,

Berger, S. & Chanko, P. *Big and Little* and *It's Spring!* Scholastic.

Bond, M. & Jankel, K. *Paddington Bear Goes to the Hospital.* HarperCollins.

Bourgeois, P. *Franklin Has a Sleepover* and The Franklin Series. Scholastic.

Bridwell, N. *Clifford the Big Red Dog* and the Clifford Series. Scholastic.

Brown, M.W. *The Runaway Bunny.* Harper.

Brown, M.W. *Goodnight Moon.* Harper & Row.

Brown, M.W. *A Child's Good Night Book.* Harper.

Burningham, J. *Mr. Gumpy's Outing.* Henry Holt & Co.

Cameron, A. *The Cat Sat on a Mat.* Houghton.

Canizares, S., & Chanko, P. *Water.* Scholastic.

Carle, E. *Do You Want to Be My Friend?* Putnam.

Carstrom, N.W. *Wild Wild Sunflower Child Anna.* Macmillan.

Clerk, J. *The Wriggly, Wriggly Baby.* Scholastic.

Cooper, H. *The Boy Who Wouldn't Go to Bed.* Dial.

Cousins, L. *The Lucy Cousins Book of Nursery Rhymes.* Dutton.

Cowell, C. *Don't Do That, Kitty Kilroy!* Scholastic.

Deming, A.G. *Who Is Tapping at My Window?* Puffin.

dePaola, T. *Tomie dePaola's Mother Goose.* Putnam.

Eastman, P.D. *Are You My Mother?* Random House.

Elliott, D. *Two Wheels for Grover.* Random House.

Falconer, I. *Olivia.* Atheneum.

Fisher Wright, B. *The Real Mother Goose Touch and Feel Book.* Scholastic.

Flack, M. *Ask Mr. Bear.* Bradbury.

Fleming, D. *Barnyard Banter.* Henry, Holt & Co.

Fox, M. *Hattie and the Fox.* Simon & Schuster.

Fox, M. *Time For Bed.* Harcourt Brace.

AGES 2–3 Books for Older Toddlers

Freedman, C. *Hushabye Lily*. Scholastic.

Freeman, D. *Corduroy Goes to the Doctor* and *Corduroy*. Viking.

Freymann, S. *Food For Thought: The Complete Book of Concepts For Growing Minds*. Scholastic.

Gliori, D. *Tickly Under There*. Scholastic.

Gomi, T. *Everyone Poops*. Kane/Miller.

Goodman, J.E. *Bernard Goes to School*. Boyd's Mill Press.

Gordon, S. *Mike's First Haircut*. Troll Associates.

Grace, W. *Red Train*. Scholastic.

Gray, K. *Eat Your Peas*. Abrams Books.

Greeley, V. *Zoo Animals*. Harper & Row.

Grimes, N. *Welcome, Precious*. Scholastic.

Guarino, D. *Is Your Mama a Llama?* Scholastic.

Gunzi, C. *My Very First Look at Numbers*. Two-Can Publishers.

Gutman, A. *Penelope Says Good Night*. Scholastic.

Henkes, K. *Owen*. Greenwillow.

Henkes, K. *So Happy!* HarperCollins.

Hill, E. *Spot's Touch and Feel Book*. Putnam.

Hughes, S. *Bathwater's Hot*. Lothrop, Lee & Shepard.

Hughes, S. *Being Together*. Candlewick Press.

Hutchins, P. *Goodnight, Owl!* Macmillan.

Ivimey, J. *Three Blind Mice*. Clarion.

Johnson, A. *Do Like Kyla* and *Rain Feet*. Scholastic.

Johnson, P.B. *On Top of Spaghetti*. Scholastic.

Juster, N. *The Hello, Goodbye Window*. Hyperion.

Keats, E. *Over in the Meadow*. Scholastic.

Kent, J. *The Fat Cat*. Scholastic.

Kirk, D. *Little Miss Spider* and *Miss Spider's ABC*. Scholastic.

Koch, M. *Hoot Howl Hiss*. Greenwillow.

Kraus, R. *Leo the Late Bloomer*. Harper Trophy.

Lamb, A. *Sam's Winter Hat*. Scholastic.

Landstrom, O. & L. *Will Gets a Haircut*. R&S Books.

Lansky, V. *Koko Bear's New Potty*. Book Peddlers.

Lawston, L. *Can You Sing?* Scholastic.

Lewison Cheyette, W. *The Princess and The Potty*. Aladdin Library.

Lewis, K. *Emma's Lamb* and *One Summer Day*. Candlewick Press.

Lindgren, B. *Sam's Potty*. William Morrow & Co.

London, J. *Froggy Gets Dressed*. Viking.

Maccarone, G. *Bless Me* and *Mother May I?* Scholastic.

Mandel, P. *Boats On the River* and *Planes at the Airport*. Scholastic.

Marshall, J. *James Marshall's Mother Goose*. Farrar.

Martin, B. *Polar Bear, Polar Bear*. Scholastic.

Marx, D.F. *Hello Doctor*. Children's Book Press.

Marzollo, J. *I Spy Little Animals* and The I Spy Series. Scholastic.

Mason, J. *Hello, Two-Wheeler*. Grosset & Dunlap.

McCourt, L. *I Love You, Stinky Face*. Scholastic.

McMullan, K. *If You Were My Bunny*. Scholastic.

McMullan, K. & J. *No, No, Jo!* Harper.

McQuade, J. *Touch the Bunny*. Scholastic.

Melser, J. *One, One, Is the Sun*. Wright.

Mitton, T. *Down by the Cool of the Pool*. Scholastic.

Moore, E. *The Day of the Bad Haircut*. Scholastic.

Morris, A. *On the Go*. Lothrop, Lee & Shepard.

Munsch, R. *Aaron's Hair*. Scholastic.

Murphy, J. *The Last Noo-Noo*. Candlewick Press.

Neubecker, R. *Beasty Bath*. Scholastic.

Noll, S. *Jiggle Wiggle Prance*. Greenwillow.

Noonan, J. *Puppy & Me: Bath Day*. Scholastic.

Numeroff, L. *If You Give A Pig A Pancake*. Scholastic.

Oxenbury, H. *Tom and Pippo and The Bicycle*. Candlewick Press.

Page, J. *Mommy Loves Her Bunny*. Scholastic.

Paparone, P. *Five Little Ducks*. Scholastic.

Paton, P. *Howard and The Sitter Surprise*. Houghton Mifflin.

Pinkney, S. *Shades of Black*. Scholastic.

Raschka, C. *Can't Sleep*. Scholastic.

Rey, H.A. *Curious George;* and Series. Houghton Mifflin.

Rohmann, E. *My Friend Rabbit*. Roaring Brook.

Root, P. *One Duck Stuck*. Candlewick Press.

Rosenberg, L. *Eli's Night-Light*. Scholastic.

Ross, A. *Elmo's Little Playhouse*. Random House.

Rueda, C. *Let's Play in the Forest*. Scholastic.

Scarry, R. *Best Word Book Ever*. Golden Press.

Schwartz, A. *A Teeny Tiny Baby*. Scholastic.

Shannon, D. *Good Boy, Fergus!* and *No, David!* Scholastic.

Skutch, R. *Who's in a Family?* Tricycle Press.

Simon, F. *Calling All Toddlers* and *Toddler Time*. Scholastic.

Slavin, B. *Cat Come Back*. Whitman.

Smalls, I. *My Pop Pop and Me*. Little, Brown Young Readers.

Sonnenschein, H. *Harold's Hideaway Thumb*. Aladdin Library.

Stockdale, S. *Carry Me! Animal Babies on the Move*. Peachtree.

Stutson, C. *Mama Loves You*. Scholastic.

Svabic, I. & Cannon, P. *No & Yes*. Scholastic.

Sweet, M. *Fiddle-I-Fee*. Little, Brown.

Tafuri, N. *I Love You, Little One; Goodnight, My Duckling; Silly Little Goose;* and *You Are Special, Little One*. Scholastic.

Tolan Brown, M. *D.W.'s Lost Blankie*. Little Brown & Company.

Valat, P.M. *First Discovery Look-Inside: Rain or Shine*. Scholastic.

Vere, E. *Everyone's Hungry, Everyone's Little,* and *Everyone's Noisy*. Scholastic.

Viorst, J. *The Good-Bye Book*. Aladdin Library.

Waber, B. *Ira Sleeps Over*. Houghton Mifflin.

Waddell, M. *Owl Babies*. Candlewick Press.

Weiss, N. *Where Does the Brown Bear Go?* Trumpet Club.

Wellington, M. *Pizza at Sally's*. Dutton.

Westcott, N.B. *Peanut Butter and Jelly*. Trumpet Club.

Weston, M. *Tuck in the Pool*. Bright Illustrations.

Whybrow, I. *The Noisy Way to Bed*. Scholastic.

Willis Hudson, C. *Let's Count, Baby*. Scholastic.

Wilson-Max, K. *Big Red Fire Truck* and *Flush The Potty!* Scholastic.

Wood, A. *The Napping House*. Harcourt.

Yee, J. *The Real Mother Goose Classic Lullaby Rhymes*. Cartwheel.

Yolen, J. *How Do Dinosaurs Learn Their Colors?* and *How Do Dinosaurs Say Good Night?* Scholastic.

Zalben, J.B. *Don't Go!* Clarion.

Ziefer, M. *Max's Potty*. DK Publication.

Ziefert, H. *No Kiss for Grandpa*. Scholastic.

Zion, G. *Harry the Dirty Dog*. Harper Collins.

Zuckerman, L. *I Will Hold You 'Til You Sleep*. Scholastic.

AGES 3–4

Andreae, G. *Giraffes Can't Dance* and *K is For Kissing a Cool Kangaroo*. Scholastic.

Arnold, T. *Huggly Takes A Bath*. Scholastic.

Arnold, T. *No Jumping On The Bed*. Dial.

Arnosky, J. *I See Animals Hiding*. Scholastic.

Aylesworth, J. *Aunt Pitty Patty's Piggy, The Gingerbread Man,* and *Goldilocks and the Three Bears*. Scholastic.

Baker, L. *I Love You Because You're You*. Scholastic.

Bang, M. *Goose*. Scholastic.

Benjamin, F. *Skip Across the Ocean: Nursery Rhymes From Around The World*. Scholastic.

Berenstain, J., & Berenstain, S. *Bears in the Night*. Random House.

Berry, M. *Up on Daddy's Shoulders*. Scholastic.

Best, C. *Are You Going to be Good?* Farrar, Straus & Giroux.

Bruss, D. *Book! Book! Book!* Scholastic.

Bunting, E. *I Love You, Too!* Scholastic.

Carle, E. *1, 2, 3, to the Zoo*. Scholastic.

Carle, E. *The Very Hungry Caterpillar*. Philomel.

Carle, E. & Iwamura, K. *Where Are You Going? To See My Friend!* Scholastic.

Cazet, D. *Night Lights – 24 Poems to Sleep on*. Scholastic.

Chase, E.N. *The New Baby Calf*. Scholastic.

Chitwood, S. *Wake Up, Big Barn*. Scholastic.

Church, C.J. *Do Your Ears Hang Low?* Scholastic.

Clifton, L. *Amifika*. E.P. Dutton.

Cohen, M. *Will I Have Friend?* Aladdin Library.

Collins, R. *Alvie Eats Soup*. Scholastic.

Cooper, E. *A Good Night Walk* and *Beach*. Scholastic.

Crews, D. *Ten Black Dots*. Harper Trohpy.

Cronin, D. *Click, Clack, Moo: Cows That Type*. Simon & Schuster.

Cronin, D. *Click, Clack, Splish Splash*. Atheneum.

Cuyler, M. *Please Play Safe! Penguin's Guide to Playground Safety* and *Please Say Please! Penguin's Guide to Manners*. Scholastic.

Davis, G. *Katy's First Haircut*. Houghton Mifflin.

Desimini, L. *Dot the Fire Dog* and *Policeman Lou and Policewoman Sue*. Scholastic.

Downey, L. *The Flea's Sneeze*. Holt.

Dunbar, J. *Where's My Sock?* Scholastic.

Ehlert, L. *A Pair of Socks*. Scholastic.

Ehlert, L. *Red Leaf, Yellow Leaf*. Harcourt.

Ehrlich, H.M. *Dancing Class*. Scholastic.

Eichenberg, F. *Ape in a Cape*. Harcourt Brace Jovanovich.

Elting, M., & Folsom, M. *Q Is for Duck*. Clarion.

Fisher Wright, B. *The Real Mother Goose Board Book* and *The Real Mother Goose*. Scholastic.

Books for Young Preschoolers

French, V. *Oliver's Milk Shake*. Scholastic.

Freymann, S. *How Are You Peeling? Foods With Moods*. Scholastic.

Galdone, P. *The Little Red Hen* and *The Three Bears*. Scholastic.

Galdone, P. *Three Little Kittens*. Clarion.

Geisert, A. *Lights Out*. Houghton Mifflin.

Gliori, D. *Flora's Blanket*. Scholastic.

Greenstein, E. *Dreaming*. Scholastic.

Goode, D. *Monkey Mo Goes to Sea*. Scholastic.

Gray, N. *A Country Far Away*. Scholastic.

Gulbis, S. *I Know an Old Lady Who Swallowed a Fly*. Scholastic.

Hall, Z. *It's Pumpkin Time!* Scholastic.

Harper, I. *My Cats Nick and Nora*. Scholastic.

Harris, P. *The Night Pirates*. Scholastic.

Ho, M. *Hush! A Thai Lullaby*. Scholastic.

Hoban, T. *26 Letters and 99 Cents*. Greenwillow.

Isaacs, A. *Pancakes for Supper*. Scholastic.

Intrater, R.G. *Two Eyes, a Nose, and a Mouth*. Scholastic.

James, B. *The Shark Who Was Afraid of Everything!* Scholastic.

Jenkins, E. *That New Animal*. Farrar, Straus & Giroux.

Johnson, A. *One of Three, Shoes Like Miss Alice's*, and *Read Me a Story, Mama*. Scholastic.

Johnson, D. *What Kind of Babysitter Is This?* Pearson Higher Education Publishing

Johnson, S.T. *Alphabet City*. Penguin.

Keats, E.J. *Regards to the Man in the Moon*. Four Winds.

Kirk, D. *Little Miss Spider at Sunny Patch School* and *Miss Spider's Tea Party*. Scholastic.

Kovalski, M. *The Wheels on the Bus*. Little, Brown.

Kuskin, K. *So, What's It Like to Be a Cat?* Simon & Schuster.

Kraus, R. *Whose Mouse Are You?* Collier.

Lamb, A. *Sam's Winter Hat*. Scholastic.

Larrañaga, A.M. *Woo! The Not-so-Scary Ghost*. Scholastic.

Lear, E. *A Was Once an Apple Pie*. Scholastic.

Lewis, K. *Dinosaur, Dinosaur*. Scholastic.

Lobel, A. *Animal Antics: A to Z* and *On Market Street*. Greenwillow.

London, J. *Froggy Learns to Swim*. Puffin.

Loomis, C. *Hattie Hippo*. Scholastic.

Low, A. *Mommy's Briefcase*. Scholastic.

Lyon, G.E. *The Outside Inn*. Scholastic.

Mack, T. *Princess Penelope Takes Charge!* Scholastic.

McCourt, L. *The Most Thankful Thing*. Scholastic.

McCourt, L. & Moore, C. *Good Night, Princess Pruney Toes*. Scholastic.

McDonald, M. *Is This a House for a Hermit Crab?* Scholastic.

McDonald, M. *Bedbugs*. Scholastic.

McGowan, S. *Pirate Girl*. Scholastic.

McLaren, C. *Zat Cat!* Scholastic.

Mendes, V. *Look at Me, Grandma*. Scholastic.

Mendez, P. *The Black Snowman*. Scholastic.

Meres, J. *The Big Bad Rumor*. Scholastic.

Metzger, S. *Five Little Sharks Swimming In the Sea*. Scholastic.

Minchella, N. *Mama Will Be Home Soon*. Scholastic.

Mitchell, M.R. *Creating Clever Castles & Cars (From Boxes and Other Stuff)*. Ideals Publication/Williamson Books.

Morgan, M. *Dear Bunny*. Scholastic.

Most, B. *Cock a Doodle Moo*. Harcourt Brace.

Munsch, R. *Alligator Baby* and *Andrew's Loose Tooth*. Scholastic.

Novak, M. *Mouse TV*. Scholastic.

Numeroff, L. *If You Give a Moose a Muffin*. Harper.

Page, J. *Let's Count*. Scholastic.

Pallotta, J. *Icky Bug Colors*. Scholastic.

Penn, A. *The Kissing Hand*. Tanglewood Press.

Pinkney, S. *Read and Rise*. Scholastic.

Pinkney, S.L. & M.C. *A Rainbow All Around Me* and *Shades of Black*. Scholastic.

Press, J. *Animal Habitats!* Ideals Publications/Williamson Books.

Raschka, C. *Yo! Yes?* Scholastic.

Rathmann, P. *Good Night, Gorilla*. Putnam.

Rex, A. *Tree Ring Circus*. Harcourt.

Riley, L. *Mouse Mess*. Scholastic.

Rockwell, A. *I Fly*. Crown Publishers.

Rogers, J. *Best Friends Sleep Over*. Scholastic.

Rollings, S. *New Shoes, Red Shoes*. Scholastic.

Rotner, S. & Calcagnino, S. *The Body Book*. Scholastic.

Rylant, C. *The Bookshop Dog* and *The Great Gracie Chase*. Scholastic.

The Scholastic First Picture Dictionary. Scholastic.

Seuss, Dr. *The Foot Book*. Random House.

Shannon, D. *Alice the Fairy, Duck on a Bike*, and *The Rain Came Down*. Scholastic.

Shaw, C. *It Looked Like Spilt Milk*. Harper.

Slepian, J. & Seidler, A. *The Hungry Thing*. Scholastic.

Smith Jr., C.R. *I Am America*. Scholastic.

Sperring, M. *Mermaid Dreams*. Scholastic.

Spowart, R. *Ten Little Bunnies*. Scholastic.

Books for Older Preschoolers

Stadler, J. *The Cats of Mrs. Calamari.* Scholastic.

Stephens, H. *Blue Horse.* Scholastic.

Stevenson, M. *A Bear for All Seasons: The Kissenbear Family Scrapbook.* Scholastic.

Sutherland, Z. (Ed.) *The Orchard Book of Nursery Rhymes.* Scholastic.

Tafuri, N. *Goodnight, My Duckling; Mama's Little Bears;* and *You Are Special, Little One.* Scholastic.

Thomas, E. *The Red Blanket.* Scholastic.

Thomas, P. *The One and Only, Super-Duper, Golly-Whopper, Jim-Dandy, Really-Handy, Clock-Tock-Stopper.* Lothrop, Lee & Shepard.

Thompson, L. *Polar Bear Night.* Scholastic.

Tolhurst, M. *Somebody and the Three Blairs.* Scholastic.

Van Leeuwen, J. *Benny and Beautiful Baby Delilah.* Penguin Putnam.

Varon, S. *Chicken & Cat.* Scholastic.

Waddell, M. *It's Quacking Time* and *Let's Go Home, Little Bear.* Candlewick Press.

Wadsworth, O.A. *Over in the Meadow.* Viking.

Watson, C. *Father Fox's Penny-Rhymes.* Scholastic.

Wells, R. *Max's Dragon Shirt.* Dial.

Wick, W. *Can You Make What I See?* Scholastic.

Wild, M. *The Pocket Dogs.* Scholastic.

Willems, M. *Time To Say Please!* Hyperion.

Winter, J. *The House That Jack Built.* Dial.

Wood, A. *Alphabet Rescue* and *The Deep Blue Sea: A Book Of Colors.* Scholastic.

Wood, A. *Quick as a Cricket.* Child's Play (International).

Wood, A. *The Napping House.* Harcourt,

Yolen, J. *How Do Dinosaurs Clean Their Rooms?, How Do Dinosaurs Eat Their Food?, How Do Dinosaurs Get Well Soon?,* and *How Do Dinosaurs Play With Their Friends?* Scholastic.

AGES 4–5

Adoff, A. *Touch the Poem.* Scholastic.

Baer, E. *This Is the Way We Go to School: A Book About Children Around the World.* Scholastic.

Bang, M. *My Light.* Scholastic.

Barrett, J. *Cloudy With a Chance of Meatballs.* Atheneum.

Bate, L. *Little Rabbit's Loose Tooth.* Joy Street Books.

Bemelmans, L. & Leaf, M. *Noodle.* Scholastic.

Best, C. *Sally Jean, The Bicycle Queen.* Farrar, Straus & Giroux

Bishop, N. *Backyard Detective: Critters Up Close.* Scholastic.

Bloom, B. *Mice Make Trouble.* Scholastic.

Blumenthal, D. *Don't Let the Peas Touch.* Scholastic.

Borden, L. *Caps, Hats, Socks, and Mittens.* Scholastic.

Brett, J. *Honey...Honey...Lion!* Penguin Putnam.

Brenner, B. (Compiler). *The Earth Is Painted Green: A Garden of Poems About Our Planet.* Scholastic.

Brown, M. *Arthur's Tooth* and Arthur Series. Joy Street Books.

Brown, M.W. *The Important Book.* Harper.

Bruchac, J. *Many Nations.* Scholastic.

Bunting, E. *Pop's Bridge.* Harcourt.

Bunting, E. *Whales Passing.* Scholastic.

Burningham, J. *Would You Rather...?* Crowell.

Carle, E. *Eric Carle's Treasury of Classic Stories for Children.* Scholastic.

Cazet, D. *Never Spit on Your Shoes.* Scholastic.

Church, C.J. *One Smart Goose.* Scholastic.

Cohen, C.L. *The Mud Pony.* Scholastic.

Cole, J. *Bony-Legs.* Scholastic.

Coombs, K. *The Secret Keeper.* Simon & Schuster.

Cowley, J. *Gracias, The Thanksgiving Turkey* and *Red-Eyed Tree Frog.* Scholastic.

Cuyler, M. *The Biggest, Best Snowman.* Scholastic.

D'Amico, C. & S. *Ella Sets the Stage.* Scholastic.

Delacre, L. *Arroz Con Leche: Popular Songs and Rhymes From Latin America.* Scholastic.

Denim, S. & Pilkey, D. *The Dumb Bunnies.* Scholastic.

dePaola, T. *The Legend of the Blue Bonnet.* Putnam.

Diakité, B.W. *The Hatseller and the Monkeys.* Scholastic.

Dillon, L. & D. *Rap A Tap Tap: Here's Bojangles–Think of That.* Scholastic.

Egan, T. *Roasted Peanuts.* Houghton Mifflin.

Feiffer, J. *I Lost My Bear.* Harper Trophy.

Fletcher, N. *See How They Grow: Penguin.* Dorling Kindersley.

Freymann, S. *One Lonely Sea Horse.* Scholastic.

Gag, W. *Millions of Cats.* Putnam.

Giovanni, N. *Rosa.* Henry Holt & Co. Books For Young Readers.

González, L.M. *The Bossy Gallito/El Gallo de Bodas.* Scholastic.

Gray, L.M. *My Mama Had a Dancing Heart.* Scholastic.

Gross, R.B. *The Bremen-Town Musicians.* Scholastic.

Gutman, A. & Hallensleben, G. *Penelope in the Winter.* Scholastic.

Henkes, K. *Lilly's Big Day.* HarperCollins Children's Books.

Hess, D. *Zen Shorts.* Scholastic.

Hesse, K. *Come on, Rain.* Scholastic.

Horenstein, H. *Arf! Beg! Catch! Dogs From A to Z.* Scholastic.

AGES 4–5 Books for Older Preschoolers

Jackson, E. *Earth Mother*. Walker Books For Young Readers.

Jackson, I. *Somebody's New Pajamas*. Dial Books.

Johnson, A. *When I Am Old With You*. Scholastic.

Johnson, P.B. *The Cow Who Wouldn't Come Down*. Scholastic.

Johnston, T. *The Iguana Brothers*. Scholastic.

Kessler, C. *The Best Beekeeper of Lalibela: A Tale From Africa*. Holiday House, Inc.

Kirk, D. *Little Miss Spider*. Scholastic.

Kraft, E. *Chocolatina*. Scholastic.

Kroll, S. *The Biggest Pumpkin Ever*. Scholastic.

Kustin, K. *Which Horse Is William?* Harper & Row.

Laguna, S. *Too Loud Lily*. Scholastic.

Lenski, L. *Sing a Song of People*. Little, Brown.

Leslie, A. *Let's Look Inside the Red Car*. Candlewick Press.

Lester, H. *Listen, Buddy*. Houghton Mifflin.

Lester, J. *What A Truly Cool World*. Scholastic.

Lionni, L. *Frederick*. Pantheon.

Lowell, S. *The Bootmaker and the Elves*. Scholastic.

Lyon, G.E. *Come a Tide*. Scholastic.

Lyons, M. *Roy Makes a Car*. Simon & Schuster.

Mack, T. *Princess Penelope*. Scholastic.

Mahy, M. *The Seven Chinese Brothers*. Scholastic.

Marzollo, J. & Wick, W. *I Spy: A Book Of Picture Riddles*. Scholastic.

McCloskey, R. *Make Way for Ducklings*. Viking.

McCourt, L. & Moore, C. *I Love You, Stinky Face*. Scholastic.

McDonald, M. *Insects Are My Life*. Scholastic.

McDonald, M. *Stink: The Incredible Shrinking Kid*. Candlewick Press.

McKissack, P.C. *Precious and the Boo Hag*. Simon & Schuster.

McMillan, B. *The Problem With Chickens*. Houghton Mifflin.

McNaughton, C. *Once Upon an Ordinary School Day*. Farrar, Straus & Giroux.

McNulty, F. *If You Decide to Go to the Moon*. Scholastic.

McQueen, L. *The Little Red Hen*. Scholastic.

Micucci, C. *The Life and Times of the Apple*. Scholastic.

Mosel, A. *Tikki Tikki Tembo*. Holt.

Munsch, R. *I'm So Embarrassed!* Scholastic.

Muntean, M. *Do Not Open This Book*. Scholastic.

Muth, J.J. *Zen Shorts*. Scholastic.

O'Conner, G. *Ker-Splash!* Simon & Schuster.

Orozco, J.L. *Rin, Rin, Rin/Do, Re, Mi*. Cartwheel Books.

Parker, K. *Counting in the Garden*. Scholastic.

Patterson, Dr. F. *Koko's Kitten*. Scholastic.

Pilkey, D. *Dog Breath*. Scholastic.

Pinkney, S. *Read and Rise*. Scholastic.

Potter, B. *The Complete Adventures of Peter Rabbit*. Wainer.

Potter, B. *The Tale of Peter Rabbit*. Scholastic.

Prelutsky, J. *Read a Rhyme, Write a Rhyme*. Random House.

Reid, B. *The Subway Mouse*. Scholastic.

Robart, R. *The Cake That Mack Ate*. Atlantic.

Rogers, J. *Tiptoe Into Kindergarten*. Scholastic.

Rose, D.L. *One Nighttime Sea*. Scholastic.

Ryan, P.M. *Mice and Beans* and *Nacho and Lolita*. Scholastic.

Schotter, R. *The Boy Who Loved Words*. Random House.

Sendak, M. *Chicken Soup With Rice*. Harper & Row.

Seuss, Dr. *Dr. Seuss's ABC*. Random House.

Sharmat, M. Gregory, *The Terrible Eater*. Scholastic.

Shelby, A. *Homeplace*. Scholastic.

Simont, M. *The Goose That Almost Got Cooked*. Scholastic.

Sklansky, A.E. *My Daddy and Me*. Scholastic.

Smith, W. *Just the Two of Us*. Scholastic.

Teague, M. *Pigsty*. Scholastic.

Vail, R. *Sometimes I'm Bombaloo*. Scholastic.

Ward, N. *Don't Eat the Teacher*. Scholastic.

Watson, R.J. *The Magic Rabbit*. Scholastic.

Wells, R. *Noisy Nora*. Dial.

Winter, J. *Frida*. Scholastic.

Wood, A. *Alphabet Adventure* and *When the Root Children Wake Up*. Scholastic.

Yolen, J. *How Do Dinosaurs Count to Ten?* and *How Do Dinosaurs Say Good Night?* Scholastic.

Yolen, J. *This Little Piggy: Lap Songs, Finger Plays, Clapping Games & Pantomime Rhymes*. Candlewick Press.

Zane, A. *The Wheels on the Race Car*. Scholastic.